MAX-PLANCK-GESELLSCHAFT

Universität
Augsburg
University

TECHNISCHE
UNIVERSITÄT
MÜNCHEN

THE GEORGE
WASHINGTON
UNIVERSITY

WASHINGTON, DC

MIPLC Studies
Edited by

Prof. Dr. Christoph Ann, LL.M. (Duke Univ.)
TUM School of Management

Prof. Robert Brauneis
The George Washington University Law School

Prof. Dr. Josef Drexl, LL.M. (Berkeley)
Max Planck Institute for Innovation and Competition

Prof. Dr. Michael Kort
University of Augsburg

Prof. Dr. Thomas M.J. Möllers
University of Augsburg

Prof. Dr. Dres. h.c. Joseph Straus
Max Planck Institute for Innovation and Competition

Volume 33

Ivan Stepanov

Eli Lilly and Beyond

The Role of International Intellectual Property Treaties
in Establishing Legitimate Expectations in Investor-State
Dispute Settlement

 **Nomos**

MIPLC Munich   Augsburg
       Intellectual München
       Property Washington DC
       Law Center

The Deutsche Nationalbibliothek lists this publication in the
Deutsche Nationalbibliografie; detailed bibliographic data
are available on the Internet at http://dnb.d-nb.de

a.t.: Munich, Master Thesis Munich Intellectual Property Law Center, 2016

ISBN   978-3-8487-5109-9 (Print)
        978-3-8452-9311-0 (ePDF)

British Library Cataloguing-in-Publication Data
A catalogue record for this book is available from the British Library.

ISBN   978-3-8487-5109-9 (Print)
        978-3-8452-9311-0 (ePDF)

Library of Congress Cataloging-in-Publication Data
Stepanov, Ivan
Eli Lilly and Beyond
The Role of International Intellectual Property Treaties in Establishing Legitimate
Expectations in Investor-State Dispute Settlement
Ivan Stepanov
84 p.
Includes bibliographic references.

ISBN   978-3-8487-5109-9 (Print)
        978-3-8452-9311-0 (ePDF)

1st Edition 2018
© Nomos Verlagsgesellschaft, Baden-Baden, Germany 2018. Printed and bound in Germany.

Foreword

This book is the adapted version of the Master thesis written in the summer of 2016 for the completion of the LL. M. program at MIPLC. The thesis is the result of my lasting interest in public international law and intellectual property law. Since its completion in September, 2016, the work has undergone some changes, primarily due to the developments in the case law it touches upon.

In the course of writing the thesis I owe thanks to many people. First of all, I am thankful to MIPLC, its directors, faculty and staff for giving me the best conditions in which I could write the thesis and thrive both academically and personally. Secondly, I thank all of my classmates for their support, love and inspiration. They have not only contributed to my academic successes but have become an important part of my personal life as well. Furthermore, I would like to thank my thesis supervisor Susan L. Karamanian for the guidance, patience and inspiration. Finally, I would like to thank my father, without whom I would not be what I am today.

6 March 2018, Munich, Germany   *Ivan Stepanov*

Table of Contents

Abstract

Through the emergence of several high-profile investment arbitration cases, the effects of IPRs as covered investments under IIAs have finally come to light. The latest award, the only arbitration case dealing with patents as IPRs – *Eli Lilly v. Canada*, has brought up a number of interesting questions. Two of Eli Lilly's patents have been revoked and the company tried to redeem them through investment arbitration. One of the claims put forward by Eli Lilly is that its legitimate expectations, a standard of protection found in international investment law, have been frustrated by Canada. By allegedly failing to observe its international IP treaty obligations contained in Chapter 17 of the NAFTA Canada frustrated Eli Lilly's legitimate expectations. In consequence of that, the thesis tries to analyze how the relationship between international IP treaties and legitimate expectations, as a standard of protection, functions. The questions which this thesis will seek to answer are the following: Can Eli Lilly, as a private person, rely on an international IP treaty, an instrument of public international law, aimed at states? To what extent are international sources of IP applicable in investment arbitration and how do they correlate with IIA protection standards like legitimate expectations?

Abbreviations and Acronyms

ADHD	Attention Deficit Hyperactive Disorder
BIT	Bilateral Investment Treaty
DSU	Dispute Settlement Understanding
ECtHR	European Court of Human Rights
FET	Fair and Equitable Treatment
FTC	NAFTA Free Trade Commission
GATS	General Agreement on Trade in Services
GATT	General Agreement on Tariffs and Trade
HRL	Human Rights Law
ICSID	International Center for Settlement of Investment Disputes
IIA	International Investment Agreements
IP	Intellectual Property
IPR	Intellectual Property Right
OECD	Organization for Economic Co-operation and Development
PCT	Patent Cooperation Treaty
PM	Philip Morris
R&D	Research and Development
SPC	Supplementary Protection Certificate
SPLT	Substantive Patent Law Treaty
TRIPS	Agreement on Trade-Related Aspects of Intellectual Property Rights
UNCITRAL	United Nations Commission on International Trade Law
UNCTAD	United Nations Conference on Trade and Development
USA/US	United States of America
VCLT	Vienna Convention on the Law of Treaties
WIPO	World Intellectual Property Organization
TPP	Trans-Pacific Partnership

I. Introduction

For years IPRs have been defined as protected investments under IIAs. And for years this relationship had been tucked away, far from the big stage of international law. However, since recently things started to change. IPRs have taken center stage in international investment arbitration with publicly available cases finally surfacing. Among them is *Eli Lilly v. Canada*,[1] a NAFTA[2] investment arbitration case. *Eli Lilly v. Canada* was the first investment arbitration case that addressed the issue of patent rights as protected investments. Eli Lilly, a US based pharmaceutical producer, had lost two of it commercially successful patents through revocation by the Canadian courts. Eli Lilly tried to redeem its lost patents through international investments proceedings, albeit unsuccessfully.[3] However among the many complex claims set forth by Eli Lilly, one of them stated that Eli Lilly's legitimate expectations, a standard of protection commonly found in international investment law, have been violated by Canada's law on the patent utility requirement for its alleged inconsistency with the relevant international IP treaty – the NAFTA IP Chapter.[4] By introducing an international IP treaty, an instrument of public international law addressed at states, into the sphere of investment arbitration, and the reach of private persons, Eli Lilly attempted to break the barriers between the two areas of law – public international law and private law. Eli Lilly asked the Tribunal to recognize its right to rely on an international IP treaty directly. Such a claim raises a number of issues. First of all, can an international IP treaty be applied in investment arbitration? If so to what extent will it be applied and how will the investment Tribunal understand it? The issues seem even more intriguing as, on the one side, IP laws

---

1 Eli Lilly & Co. v. Canada, ICSID, Case No. UNCT/14/2 (2012), available at: http://www.italaw.com/cases/1625 (Visited last on Mar. 6, 2018) [herein after: *Eli Lilly v. Canada*].

2 North American Free Trade Agreement, U.S.-Can.-Mex., Dec. 17, 1992, 32 I.L.M. 289 (1993) [hereinafter NAFTA].

3 *Eli Lilly v. Canada,* Supra note 1, Final Award, available at: https://www.italaw.com/sites/default/files/case-documents/italaw8546.pdf (Visited last on Mar. 6, 2018) [herein after: Final Award].

4 NAFTA, Supra note 2, Chap. 17.

are carefully crafted by the state to suit its domestic goals and policies. On the other side are investment Tribunals who have their own purpose and understanding of the law. Behind this seemingly dry legalistic problem a much bigger background emerges. IPRs are tools of policy and are recognized as such on an international level.[5] By placing IPRs and international IP treaties into the system of international investment law and arbitration there is a risk that the delicately crafted policy objectives become disrupted by the broad protection standards found in IIAs, such as legitimate expectations. However, investment Tribunals can hardly be prevented from exercising their powers, which might include assessing and applying international IP treaties as the relevant law. As jurisprudence on the matter is still developing and academic writing having only recently started addressing this issue, it remains unclear how the Tribunals will address the legal and policy measures with IPRs as their object. This remains true even after the award was rendered by the Tribunal, as it never actually debated the issue.

This thesis will try to show that investment Tribunals nevertheless have limited interpretation space, mostly stemming from the wording of IIAs and to an extent from the rules of international IP treaties themselves. Furthermore, the thesis will attempt at demonstrating, should the investment Tribunals be consistent with the current jurisprudence and take the appropriate approach in applying the law, the policy flexibilities offered by international IP treaties should nevertheless be left unfettered. A two-fold approach will be taken. Firstly, the specific relationship of international IP treaties and legitimate expectations in the *Eli Lilly v. Canada* case itself will be analyzed. Secondly a broader analysis, that is outside of the specific scope of the NAFTA, will be conducted by applying the principles derived from the case onto a global legal environment. The thesis will be structured in the following manner. Chapter II will set out the international legal framework. It will introduce the relevant international treaties and shortly survey their characteristics important for the analysis. A part of the chapter will be devoted to the protection of IPRs in international investment law. Chapter III will present the background and the summary of the relevant facts from the *Eli Lilly v. Canada* case. The emphasis will be on the argumentation relevant to the claim of basing legitimate expectations

---

5 Ruth L. Okediji, Is Intellectual Property "Investment"? Eli Lilly v. Canada and the International Intellectual Property System, 35 U. Pa. J. Int'l L. 1211, 1226&1133 (2013-2014).

in the NAFTA IP Chapter. Chapter IV will present the "promise utility doctrine", the contentious legal doctrine pivotal to the case. The doctrine will be reflected against the backdrop of Canadian patent law. The chapter will conclude with a small analysis regarding the consistency of the doctrine with international IP standards. Chapter V will address two major areas. It will try to explain the FET standard and legitimate expectations as its constituent part. The focus will be on NAFTA investment arbitration case law which will be relevant for assessing the relationship of international IP treaties in establishing legitimate expectations. The chapter will conclude with the observation of the two recent investment law cases that have addressed the issue of legitimate expectations and IPRs. Chapter VI will attempt at giving an analysis of the validity and possible success of the claim. A parallel analysis will be attempted with a focus on the broader legal environment of IPRs and international investment law. Chapter VI will address the issues of using policy justification for changes in IP legislation pertaining to the defense in investment arbitration. The thesis will conclude with a small summary and a few general recommendations.

II. International Legal Framework

A. *International Intellectual Property Law*

1. International Intellectual Property Treaties

The first multilateral treaties that addressed the issues of IP and obliged the states to create basic IPRs in their legal systems were the Paris Convention[6] and the Berne Convention.[7] The two treaties are deemed to be the cornerstone treaties of what can generally be called international IP law.[8] Established at the end of the 19th century the treaties were created as a response to unwarranted business practices in the modern world, whose economy was increasingly reliant on knowledge. The idea behind the treaties was to grant protection to innovators and artist, in particular writers, with a view of incentivizing creation and innovation.[9] From a purely legislative perspective the treaties created a set of legal standards to be implemented by the states. The cornerstone of both treaties is the national treatment standard. In addition, the Paris convention expressly contained the most favored nation principle.[10] These provisions provided for a fair amount of legal harmonization internationally, without creating too much obligations in the treaties themselves. Interestingly, the Paris convention did not create wide substantive rights. The treaty mainly addressed procedural and formal aspects of industrial property law.[11] Quite notably there was no obligation to introduce patent protection in domestic law. Like-

---

6 Paris Convention for the Protection of Industrial Property, Mar. 20, 1883, 21 U.S.T. 1583, 828 U.N.T.S. 305 [herein after: Paris Convention].

7 Berne Convention for the Protection of Literary and Artistic Works, Sep. 9, 1886, 331 U.N.T.S. 217, [herein after: Bern Convention].

8 DANIEL GERVAIS, THE TRIPS AGREEMENT: DRAFTING HISTORY AND ANALYSIS, 3rd ed., § 1.10 (2008).

9 Rochelle Dreyfuss & Susy Frankel, FROM INCENTIVE TO COMMODITY TO ASSET: HOW INTERNATIONAL LAW IS RECONCEPTUALIZING INTELLECTUAL PROPERTY, 36 Mich. J. Int'l L. 557, 561 (2014-2015).

10 Paris Convention, Supra note 6, art. 3 and 4, and Bern Convention, Supra note 7, art. 5(3)

11 For example, it provides the right of the inventor to be mentioned (Paris Convention art. 4ter), priority period rules for patent registration in multiple countries

wise, there were no provisions stipulating the establishment or setting of patentability requirements. These matters were left to the states to implement on their own accord. The legislative gaps assured that state sovereignty was recognized with considerable room left for the introduction of measures benefiting their own domestic goals. Moreover, neither treaty had a strong compliance mechanism, which resulted in no complaints ever being filled on an international level.[12] Over the years both treaties were amended in order to adapt to modern times and practices.[13]

After the Second World War social changes accelerated worldwide. The developments in politics, trade and technology created new paradigms in international economic relations and IP along with it.[14] Politically the facilitation of free trade was seen as a way to ensure peace after the War. Out of that idea the GATT[15] was born. GATT created a legal framework for the free flow of goods.[16] Following in the next few decades, the development of the IT sector and the emergence of the internet created unprecedented business opportunities. Things were changing rapidly and IP was becoming increasingly relevant in the world economy.[17] This meant that its prominence had risen in the political debate as well. IP right holders started requesting that a precise definition of IPRs be provided so as to accommodate the needs of their international business models. The attention turned to WIPO, the caretaker of the major IP treaties. WIPO was asked to adapt the rules on IP to the newly developed circumstances. However, this attempt failed. From there the focus shifted to WTO and as a result the TRIPS was created.[18] The shift brought in considerable changes in all IP fields. Conceptually IP started being perceived primarily as a constituent

---

(Paris Convention art. 4) and the conditions for the issuance of compulsory licenses (Paris Convention art. 5).

12 Dreyfuss & Frankel, Supra note 9, at 562.

13 The Paris Convention was amended 7 times from 1900 to 1979 and the Bern Convention was amended 8 times from 1886 to 1979.

14 Peter Van Den Bossche, The Law and Policy of the World Trade Organization, 2nd ed., 5 (2010).

15 1994: General Agreement on Tariffs and Trade 1994, Apr. 15, 1994, Marrakesh Agreement Establishing the World Trade Organization, Annex 1A, THE LEGAL TEXTS: THE RESULTS OF THE URUGUAY ROUND OF MULTILATERAL TRADE NEGOTIATIONS 17 (1999), 1867 U.N.T.S. 187.

16 Ralph H. Folsom, Principles of International Trade Law, 7 (2014).

17 Dreyfuss & Frankel, Supra note 9, at 562.

18 Peter Drahos with John Braithwaite, Information Feudalism, Who Owns the Knowledge Economy, 61-62 (2002).

part of international trade and IPRs started being viewed as rights proper. IP assumed the shape of commodities,[19] a far cry from IP known in the 19th century.

The TRIPS is one of the main agreements that forms a part of what is known as WTO law. It is a comprehensive agreement that in great detail deals with a multitude of IPR aspects. First of all, it obliges the states to introduce protection for IPRs and determines the minimum standards which IPRs need to be subject to. The state is notably allowed to implement higher standards but that is left to the state's discretion.[20] The TRIPS provides for the incorporation of the Paris and Berne treaties as integral parts of the TRIPS.[21] The principles of most favored nation and national treatment likewise found their ways into the treaty.[22] Furthermore the TRIPS creates a set of substantive rights that the states are required to implement. This is a significant development in comparison to the two other major IP treaties mentioned previously, where no such obligations existed. Express language that creates these standards and sets the scopes of protection can be found in the TRIPS. For example, article 27(1)[23] states: "[s]ubject to the provisions of paragraphs 2 and 3, patents shall be available for any inventions, whether products or processes, in all fields of technology, provided that they are new, involve an inventive step and are capable of industrial application." The TRIPS also provides a minimum set of rights that should be conferred to the right holders. For copyright protection minimum rights were already established in the Bern Convention.[24] However the Paris Convention provided much less in terms of the minimum of rights afforded to the right holders. The TRIPS article 27 creates two essential rights for patent holders – the right to exclude other

---

19 Laurinda L. Hicks & James R. Holbein, CONVERGENCE OF NATIONAL INTELLECTU- AL PROPERTY NORMS IN INTERNATIONAL TRADING AGREEMENTS, 2 Am. U.J. Int'l L. & Pol'y, 769, 770 (1997).

20 Agreement on Trade-Related Aspects of Intellectual Property Rights, Apr. 15, 1994, Marrakesh Agreement Establishing the World Trade Organization, Annex 1C, THE LEGAL TEXTS: THE RESULTS OF THE URUGUAY ROUND OF MULTILATERAL TRADE NEGOTIATIONS 320 (1999), 1869 U.N.T.S. 299, 33 I.L.M. 1197 (1994) [herein after: TRIPS].

21 *Id*, art. 2.

22 *Id*, art. 3 & 4.

23 *Id*, art. 27.

24 Bern Convention, Supra note 5, art. 6-19.

from using the patents (the so called negative right),[25] and the right to transfer or license the patent to others.[26] The TRIPS expressly recognizes possible variations in the scope and nature of protection. Article 27(3) for example envisages the possibility of exclusion of certain types of inventions from patenting. Article 6 excludes the application of the most favored nation and national treatment to the law dealing with international IP exhaustion.[27] Furthermore concepts found in article 9 like 'expression' and 'idea' or 'new',[28] 'inventive step' and 'industrial application' found in article 27 are left undefined at the treaty level.[29] Another significant development found in TRIPS is the enforcement part.[30] This part of the treaty sets precise obligations for the state in regards to the enforcement of IP rights. Not only does it secure a general enforcement framework[31] but it likewise provides more detailed obligations on damages, injunctions, criminal penalties and evidence.[32] The TRIPS, even though providing a substantial amount of obligations for WTO member states, leaves some regulatory leeway for the implementation of the rules. This is achieved by omitting strict definitions of treaty terms[33] and giving the chance to exclude certain types of protection.[34] The TRIPS likewise recognizes the non-absolute nature of IPRs by providing rules for certain limitations of rights. The compulsory license's rules or the three-step test exception are prime examples thereof.[35] These international rules are constructed to leave policy space for their implementation at the domestic level. In that regard the TRIPS is not only a purely legal document but it holds significance in a political and diplomatic sense as well. However, the TRIPS was

---

25 TRIPS, Supra note 20, art. 28(1).
26 *Id*, art. 28(2).
27 *Id*, art. 6.
28 *Id*, art. 9.
29 *Id*, art. 27.
30 *Id*, part III.
31 *Id*, art. 41.
32 *Id*, art. 43-46.
33 For example, TRIPS art. 27(1) contains the terms invention, new, inventive step, industrial application without ascribing any definitive meaning to them.
34 TRIPS, Supra note 20, art. 27(3).
35 *Id*, art. 30 & 31.

already a policy concession for some countries[36]. It was adopted as a tradeoff for access to other economic areas and it is considered a compromise even in some developed countries.[37] Nevertheless states often followed their own approach to the implementation of the TRIPS rules. The difference in how the TRIPS was perceived from a national perspective resulted in different implementations of the TRIPS norms in domestic legal systems.

With the TRIPS being part of the WTO *acquis*, the enforcement of IPRs is not only secured in national legal orders but from an international law perspective as well. This means that the states' compliance with their international law obligations is secured through the WTO dispute settlement mechanism. So far there have been 37 registered cases before the WTO dispute settlement system arising out of the TRIPS agreement.[38] Cases such as *Canada — Patent Term*[39] and *United States — Section 110(5) of US Copyright Act*[40] are prominent examples how the TRIPS flexibilities function.

The *Canada — Patent Term* case dealt with two measures implemented by the Canadian government on the stockpiling and the regulatory review of soon-to-expire pharmaceutical patents. With these measures the Canadian government wanted to speed up the appearance of generic drugs on the market. The Canadian government legislated certain exemptions in the patent legislation which affected some patents preceding the date of their expiry. The WTO panel concluded that the regulatory review was an ex-

---

36 States were obliged to provide patent protection even if they did not have it before. SOUTH CENTER, THE TRIPS AGREEMENT, A GUIDE FOR THE SOUTH, THE URUGUAY ROUND AGREEMENT ON TRADE-RELATED INTELLECTUAL PROPERTY RIGHTS, 19 (2000).

37 Anthony Taubman, AUSTRALIA'S INTERESTS UNDER TRIPS DISPUTE SETTLEMENT: TRADE NEGOTIATIONS BY OTHER MEANS, MULTILATERAL DEFENSE OF DOMESTIC POLICY CHOICE, OR SAFEGUARDING MARKET ACCESS?, 9 Melb. J. Int'l L. 217, 222 (2008).

38 For a list of cases see, https://www.wto.org/english/tratop_e/dispu_e/dispu_agreements_index_e.htm?id=A26# (Visited last on Mar. 6, 2018).

39 *Panel Report, Canada – Term of Patent Protection,* WT/DS170/AB/R, (Oct. 12, 2000) [herein after: *Canada – Patent Term*].

40 *Panel Report, United States-Section 110(5) of the U.S. Copyright Act,* WT/DS160/R (Jun. 15, 2000) [herein after: *US – Copyright Act Section 110(5)*].

emption that was allowed, while the stockpiling exemption was not.[41] In the *United States — Section 110(5) of US Copyright Act* case the exemptions for the payment of royalties coming from a certain type of small hospitality establishment. Namely restaurants of a certain size were exempt from paying copyright and related rights' royalties. This exemption was found to be inconsistent with WTO law.[42] However interestingly the US never actually implemented the recommendation evidenced by the provision still standing today.[43] The two cases shed light on several aspects of the TRIPS. They show how the WTO dispute settlement mechanism uses the TRIPS in determining limits and exception of IPRs. They likewise show the TRIPS used in such a way that it is not a pure adversarial, litigation like tool for settling disputes. As part of international law, it is subject to politics and diplomacy. Even when the norm might not be TRIPS compliant it is up to the state to decide how to act on it.[44]

Another function that can be attributed to the TRIPS is its perceived function and use as a benchmark for IP law, a policy guide and "ghostwriter" for domestic legislators.[45] However the TRIPS leaves much to be desired for the private person. All aspects of WTO law remain in the sphere of public international law. As such the recourse to the dispute settlement mechanism is left strictly to the states. Therefore, in case private parties wish to raise a TRIPS violation complaint, they must persuade a WTO Member State government to do it for them. Due to the political and diplomatic dimension of the TRIPS the states might therefore be reluctant to pursue conflict resolution through this method. Another reason for this is that the states might rely on domestic legal provisions which are borderline compliant with WTO law and are unwilling do endanger themselves through possible retributive proceedings.[46]

---

41 See, *Canada – Patent Term,* Summary available at https://www.wto.org/english/ tratop_e/dispu_e/cases_e/1pagesum_e/ds114sum_e.pdf (Visited last on Mar. 6, 2018).
42 See, *US – Copyright Act Section 110(5)*, Summary available at https:// www.wto.org/english/tratop_e/dispu_e/cases_e/1pagesum_e/ds160sum_e.pdf (Visited last on Mar. 6, 2018).
43 Copyright Act of 1976 § 110 (5)(B)(i), 17 U.S.C., § 107 (2012)
44 See Taubman, Supra note 37, 230-31.
45 *Id,* at 222, 227.
46 Valentina Vadi, Towards a New Dialectics: Pharmaceutical Patents, Public Health and Foreign Direct Investment, 5(1) NYU J. Intell. Prop. & Ent. L., 113, 141 (2015).

B. International Investment Law

1. International Investment Agreements

IIAs are international treaties signed between states, usually in bilateral or on rarer occasions multilateral form, whose purpose is to secure a stable investment framework for foreign investors.[47] The root of IIAs lies in the reciprocal arrangements of European nations which offered protection to foreign owned property.[48] The early international investment agreements signed in the post Second World War period were based on the Friendship, Navigation and Commerce treaties from the nineteenth century.[49] The first modern IIA is considered to be the Germany – Pakistan Bilateral Investment Treaty of 1959.[50] Nowadays there are more than 3000 IIAs worldwide.[51] The idea behind these agreements was to stimulate the flow of foreign direct investment to countries that desired foreign capital on the one side. On the other side, their aim was to provide security to the investors against the disturbance and confiscation of their assets. The presumption was that the countries needing foreign capital do not always possess the required legal stability. The protection was therefore secured by incorporating many different types of property and assets under the definition of investment.[52] The standards of protection such as the FET standard and the rules on expropriation were defined broadly, with the intent of covering as many potential situations as possible. The idea was to provide the in-

---

47 *The Role of International Investment Agreements in Attracting Foreign Direct Investment to Developing Countries*, UNCTAD Series on International Investment Policies for Development, 14-15 (2009).

48 Kate Miles, THE ORIGINS OF INTERNATIONAL INVESTMENT LAW, EMPIRE, ENVIRONMENT AND THE SAFEGUARDING OF CAPITAL, 21 (2013).

49 Margie-Lys Jaime, RELYING UPON PARTIES' INTERPRETATION IN TREATY-BASED INVESTOR-STATE DISPUTE SETTLEMENT: FILLING THE GAPS IN INTERNATIONAL INVESTMENT AGREEMENTS, 46 Geo. J. Int'l L., 261, 266 (2014-2015).

50 Treaty between the Federal Republic of Germany and Pakistan for the Promotion and Protection of Investment, Ger. - Pak., Nov. 25, 1959, 457 U.N.T.S. 24 [hereinafter: Germany – Pakistan BIT].

51 Valentina Sara Vadi, THROUGH THE LOOKING-GLASS: INTERNATIONAL INVESTMENT LAW THROUGH THE LENS OF PROPERTY THEORY, 8 Manchester J. Int'l Econ. L., 22, 33 (2011).

52 Stephanie Bijlmakers, EFFECTS OF FOREIGN DIRECT INVESTMENT ARBITRATION ON A STATE'S REGULATORY AUTONOMY INVOLVING THE PUBLIC INTEREST, 23 Am. Rev. Int'l Arb., 245, 253 (2012).

vestors with wide recourse options for the protection of their invest-ments.[53]

Even though IIAs can be drafted differently as regard the form and scope of protection, several recurring parts can still be distinguished. The US Model BIT[54] will be used as a showpiece treaty for the purpose of this thesis. The first general section is the "definitions" section. These provi-sions clarify and give interpretative meaning to the substance of the treaty. Perhaps the most important part of this section is the definition of *the in-vestment*.[55] The definition is crucial as terms not covered by the definition do not fall under the treaty's scope of protection, hence there is no juris-diction *ratione materiae*. The second section provides a number of sub-stantive rights to the investors. Protection through the FET standard, rules on justifiable expropriation or the rules on the free flow of capital are all commonly found in IIAs.[56] The third section prescribes the acceptable state behavior by stipulating obligations requiring abstinence from certain actions. The section likewise stipulates the creation of the exceptions in favor of the state.[57] Finally the last major section creates a possibility for the investor, a private person, to seek direct recourse against the host state if it deems that the host state had violated rights provided by the treaty which likewise resulted in the investor suffering economic damage. The recourse sought is found in the form of investor-state dispute settlement, or colloquially called (international) investment arbitration.[58]

2. International Investment Arbitration

International investment arbitration is a dispute settlement mechanism which grants access to the investor, a private person, to challenge mea-

---

53 Jaime, Supra note 49, at 269.
54 2012 U.S. Model Bilateral Investment Treaty, Treaty Between The Government of the United States of America and the Government Of [Country] Concerning The Encouragement and Reciprocal Protection of Investment, available at: http://www.state.gov/documents/organization/188371.pdf (Visited last on Mar. 6, 2018) [herein after: US Model BIT].
55 *Id,* art. 1.
56 *Id,* art. 5-7.
57 *Id.* art. 10-13.
58 *Id.* art. 24.

sures of the state if it deems that its treaty rights had been violated.[59] This mechanism intends to secure a balance between the rights of the investor with the state's right to regulate.[60] Unlike the older IP treaties which had no embedded dispute settlement mechanisms[61] or the WTO's which grants access only to the states,[62] IIAs give access to a private person to challenge the state directly in an international dispute settlement forum.[63] As in other types of arbitration there is a possibility to choose the applicable arbitration rules that will govern the investment arbitration proceedings. Some are investment arbitration specific,[64] while others that are designed for commercial arbitration, in general, are likewise applicable.[65] Investment arbitration awards are accordingly recognized and enforced through the New York Convention.[66]

However, investment arbitration is nowadays under criticism. The considerable power conferred to investment Tribunals is not seen in a positive light.[67] They are deemed holding absolutist views of property with little regard for other values.[68] Likewise the chance for the investor to challenge a state's regulatory measure, particularly ones pertaining to human rights, the environment and public health has raised considerable concerns.[69] The sheer possibility of challenging national legislation, which need not materialize in practice, can often lead to the "regulatory chill." In practice this

---

59 Not all IIAs have this option. For example, the Germany – Pakistan BIT art. 11 provides only for state to state arbitration in case of a dispute in the interpretation of the treaty.

60 Jaime, Supra note 49, at 269.

61 Dreyfuss & Frankel, Supra note 9, at 562.

62 Referring to "Members" which are states. Understanding on Rules and Procedures Governing the Settlement of Disputes, Marrakesh Agreement Establishing the World Trade Organization, Annex 2, THE LEGAL TEXTS: THE RESULTS OF THE URUGUAY ROUND OF MULTILATERAL TRADE NEGOTIATIONS 354 (1999), 1869 U.N.T.S. 401, art. 1. [herein after: DSU].

63 US Model BIT, Supra note 54, art. 24.

64 For example, International Centre for Settlement of Investment Disputes (ICSID), Rules of Procedure for the Institution of Conciliation and Arbitration Proceedings, Mar. 18, 1965, ICSID/15/Rev. 1 (2003) [herein after: ICSID Rules].

65 For example, UNCITRAL Arbitration Rules, Dec. 15, 1976, 15 I. L. M. 701 (1976); [herein after: UNCITRAL Rules].

66 Convention on the Recognition and Enforcement of Foreign Arbitral Awards, Jun 10, 1958, 330 UNTS 38.

67 Bijlmakers, Supra note 52, at 253.

68 Vadi, Supra note 51, at 30.

69 Bijlmakers, Supra note 52, at 254.

means that states threatened by possible investment arbitration might often be reluctant to change their own laws.[70] It seems the criticism has nevertheless to some degree been fruitful. Nowadays investment Tribunals show more deference to the state's right to regulate.[71] This has not however ever deterred investors trying to challenge the state's regulatory mechanisms.

3. Intellectual Property Rights as Protected Investments

It is generally accepted that IPRs can be protected as investments. This coverage finds its basis in the "definitions" part of an IIA. IPRs can therefore be covered by being directly named or by using the terms such as "intangible property".[72] However the broad and loose definition does not necessarily encapsulate all of the aspects of IPRs. IPRs have some distinct features in comparison with the classical notion of property or rights usually covered in international investments law. IPRs are territorial in nature. What constitutes a patent and consequently a protected investment in one country, might be denied patent protection in another, thus affording no investment law protection to the same invention. As some IPRs are acquired through registration an unsuccessful registration will not confer investment protection.[73] Beyond the matter of providing protection to IPRs as investments, the relationship between the special characteristics of IPRs[74] and the standards of protection[75] commonly found in IIAs remains very much in the air. Ultimately the ability to determine what are IPRs and to what extent they are protected is left to the state.[76] The protection of

---

70 JOHNATHAN GRIFFITHS, ON THE BACK OF A CIGARETTE PACKET: STANDARDIZED PACKAGING LEGISLATION AND THE TOBACCO INDUSTRY'S FUNDAMENTAL RIGHT TO INTELLECTUAL PROPERTY, 4 I. P. Q. 243, 245 (2015).
71 Bijlmakers, Supra note 52, at 254 & Vadi, Supra note 51, at 31.
72 Bryan Mercurio, AWAKENING THE SLEEPING GIANT: INTELLECTUAL PROPERTY RIGHTS IN INTERNATIONAL INVESTMENT AGREEMENTS, 15 (3) J. Int't Econ. L., 871, 874-76 (2012).
73 *Id.,* at 876-78.
74 For example, compulsory licenses in patents or the existence of the right to exclude in contrast with the right to use in patents and trademarks.
75 The FET standard protection and rules on expropriation.
76 Tania Voon, Andrew Mitchell & James Munro, INTELLECTUAL PROPERTY RIGHTS IN INTERNATIONAL INVESTMENT AGREEMENTS: STRIVING FOR COHERENCE IN NATIONAL AND INTERNATIONAL LAW, (Melbourne Legal Studies Research Paper,

IPRs should therefore be observed in line with the legislation of the state. The role of IIAs should hence be to confirm the existing rights which are created in domestic law.[77] An approach which can have some merit in investment arbitration is the one taken by the ECtHR. In a case relating to an IPR the Court recognized the right of domestic courts to clarify and interpret the scope of IPRs.[78] The protection of IPRs, which are not absolute in their nature,[79] under IIAs should be acknowledge in full, with all the rights and limitations included.[80] This is particularly important as IPRs are used as policy tools in many ways. The scope of protection alongside with the limitations of rights are crafted to serve exactly that purpose.

C. NAFTA

The NAFTA is an agreement signed by the USA, Canada and Mexico in an effort to liberalize and facilitate trade, while also eliminating barriers for investment in North America.[81] Being a comprehensive agreement the NAFTA not only provides rules regarding the trade in goods, but likewise the rules on trade in services[82] and the rules on technical barriers to trade[83]. The treaty also creates bodies in charge of administering the treaty, like the FTC[84] and the rules for inter-partes dispute settlement[85]. However

---

Paper No. 675, 2013), 1, 8 http://papers.ssrn.com/sol3/papers.cfm?abstract_id=2318955 (Visited last on Mar. 6, 2018).

77 Okediji, Supra note 5, at 1219.

78 Griffiths, Supra note 70, at 355.

79 Vadi, Supra note 46, at 195.

80 In one of the drafts of the TPP the following phrase was used when defining intellectual property rights as investments: "intellectual property rights [which are conferred pursuant to domestic law" see, Brook K. Baker & Katrina Geddes, CORPORATE POWER UNBOUND: INVESTOR-STATE ARBITRATION OF IP MONOPOLIES ON MEDICINES – ELI LILLY V. CANADA AND THE TRANS-PACIFIC PARTNERSHIP AGREEMENT, (Northeastern Pub. Law and Legal Theory Faculty Research Paper Ser., Paper No. 242, 2015), 1, 22 http://papers.ssrn.com/sol3/papers.cfm?abstract_id=2667062 (Visited last on Mar. 6, 2018).

81 ROBERT A. PASTOR, THE NORTH AMERICAN IDEA, THE VISION OF A CONTINENTAL FUTURE, 7-9 (2011).

82 NAFTA, Supra note 2, Chap. 12-14.

83 *Id.* Chap. 9.

84 *Id.* Chap. 18

85 *Id.* Chap. 19

particularly important for this thesis are two chapters – the IP Chapter[86] and the Investment Chapter.[87]

The NAFTA IP Chapter, is structured in a similar fashion to the TRIPS, although in certain instances it is more extensive. The Chapter when enacted mostly impacted Mexican IP law but the US and Canada needed to amend their legislation as well.[88]

The NAFTA Investment Chapter was enacted to liberalizes foreign direct investment particularly in Mexico, which had a closed and controlled system for foreign investment. Nowadays the NAFTA is one of the most commonly used investment arbitration mechanisms.[89] The Investment Chapter creates substantive rules intended for foreign investors in the similar to other IIAs. Provision establishing the FET standard[90] or the rules on the expropriation of investments[91] are clear examples thereof. Furthermore, the Chapter creates the option for investor-state dispute settlement.[92] The dispute resolution mechanism is set out in considerable detail and provides extensive guidance for all procedural aspects of investment arbitration. One of the most important provisions of the dispute resolution section is article 1139. In this article the definition of what should be or should not be considered an investment is given. The language of sub-paragraph 1139 (g) provides that "[i]nvestment means real estate or other property, tangible or intangible, acquired in the expectation or used for the purpose of economic benefit or other business purposes." Even though not expressly mentioned, IPRs, being intangible rights, can be covered as investments.[93] The provision lays the cornerstone of any claim by the investor based on the perceived mistreatment of IPRs by the state. The perceived mistreatment of those rights will be assessed from the law applicable to investment arbitration. This means that the actions of the state will be subject to the evaluation under the FET standard (article 1105) and the

---

86 *Id.* Chap. 17
87 *Id.* Chap. 11
88 RALPH. H. FOLSOM, NAFTA, FREE TRADE AND FOREIGN INVESTMENT IN THE AMERICAS IN A NUTSHELL, 199 (2014)
89 Vanessa Humm, AMERICAN TRADE NEWS HIGHLIGHTS FOR SUMMER 2013, THE RISE OF THE INVESTOR – STATE SUIT AND THE CALL FOR REFORM, 5 Law & Bus. Rev. Am. 425, 427 (2013)
90 NAFTA, Supra note 2, art. 1105
91 NAFTA, Supra note 2, art. 1110
92 NAFTA, Supra note 2, art. 1115-1139
93 Mercurio, Supra note 72, at 874-76.

rules on expropriation (article 1110). However little guidance is given how inherent limitations of IPRs correspond with the Investment Chapter. The only reference to IPRs is found in article 1110(7). The article states that compulsory licenses and the creation, limitation or creation of IPRs, if done in accordance with the NAFTA IP Chapter cannot constitute expropriation. However, further elaboration on the relationship between article 1105 and the IP chapter is left undefined. Another notable provision, that sheds light on the relationship of the NAFTA Investment Chapter with the rest of the treaty, is article 1112 which essentially subordinates the whole NAFTA Investment Chapter to the rest of the NAFTA treaty.[94]

---

94 Ralph. H. Folsom, Supra note 86, at 171.

III. Eli Lilly v. Canada – Facts and Proceedings

The case central to the analysis of this thesis is the investment arbitration case between Eli Lilly, a US pharmaceutical company and the government of Canada. Eli Lilly was the proprietor of two pharmaceutical patents for commercially successful drugs called Strattera and Zyprexa. Both of the patents were revoked in court proceedings after being challenged by competing generic producers. Having lost both cases in the final court instance Eli Lilly started the investment arbitration proceedings under NAFTA Investment Chapter in 2012. The proceedings were conducted according to the UNCITRAL Rules.[95]

A. Eli Lilly's Patents in Canadian Courts

1. Strattera Patent

The Strattera patent was a patent for a new use of an already known substance called atomoxetine, a drug used to treat manifestation of ADHD.[96] The patent was challenged on the grounds for the lack of utility by Novopharm, now Teva Canada, a generic pharmaceutical producer.

The trial judge found that, at the time of the filing of the patent, the evidence provided by Eli Lilly did not suffice to show that atomoxetine would fulfill the promise disclosed in the patent.[97] The judge determined that the clinical study used as evidence of the utility of the patent was not enough to establish a promise of utility at the time of the filing.[98] The decision was latter appealed to the Supreme Court of Canada, which refused to hear it. With that Eli Lilly exhausted all recourse to domestic courts.[99]

---

95 UNCITRAL Rules, Supra note 65.
96 Eli Lilly & Co. v. Teva Canada Ltd., § 2, [2011] FCA 220, [herein after: *Eli Lilly v. Teva*].
97 *Id*, § 5.
98 *Id.*, §§ 34-40.
99 Eli Lilly & Co v. Teva Canada Ltd., [2011] Supreme Court No. 34396, (Can.), available at: https://scc-csc.lexum.com/scc-csc/scc-l-csc-a/en/item/8970/index.do (Visited last on Mar. 6, 2018).

2. Zyprexa Patent

The Zyprexa patent was a selection patent for a previously patented substance called olanzapine. Olanzapine is used for the treatment of schizophrenia.[100] The patent holders claimed: "[w]e have now discovered a compound which possesses surprising and unexpected properties by comparison with flumezapine and other related compounds". Such a disclosure pointed to the advantages of the previously known substance.[101] The patent itself was attacked on two grounds - the lack of utility and insufficient disclosure. While the insufficiency of disclosure claim was rejected, the utility claim was nevertheless successful.[102] The court found that the evidence presented did not prove the marked advantages of olanzapine over the rest of the patent genus.[103] Moreover the court found that the evidence submitted did not establish a prediction needed to fulfill the promise of utility.[104]

The decision was appealed and eventually dismissed by the Supreme Court of Canada.[105]

The reasoning for the revocation of both patents is very similar. The courts found that the utility of the patent could not have been demonstrated at the moment of filing, nor that any indication of utility was demonstrated at the same time. Based on pure speculation, the patents were revoked for their lack of utility.[106]

Dissatisfied with the outcome of the court proceedings Eli Lilly decided to start an investment arbitration against Canada according to the NAFTA Investment Chapter. The case would become the first, publicly available investor-state arbitration dealing with patent rights as investment. Eli Lilly caught on with the trend of large companies trying to challenge domestic

---

100 Eli Lilly & Co. v. Novopharm Ltd., § 1, [2011] FC 1288 (Can.) [herein after: *Eli Lilly v. Novopharm*].

101 *Id,* §§ 32 – 36.

102 *Id,* § 7.

103 *Id,* § 73.

104 *Id,* §§ 74-78.

105 Eli Lilly & Co. v. Novopharm Ltd., Supreme Court No. 35067 (Can.) available at: https://scc-csc.lexum.com/scc-csc/scc-l-csc-a/en/item/13052/index.do (Visited last on Mar. 6, 2018).

106 James Billingsley, Eli Lilly and Company v. The Government of Canada and the Perils of Investor-State Arbitration, 20 Appeal 27, 30 (2015).

IP law through shifting the forum to investor-state arbitration.[107] A view exists which posits that investment arbitration Tribunals have an investment-centered approach and have a different perspective when it comes to observing property rights.[108] The idea behind Lilly's actions was that through forum shifting it would be possible to mitigate the negative consequences of domestic law or judicial decisions. Although Lilly lost the case and the battle[109], one could say that they still won the war, as the Supreme Court of Canada eventually struck out the promise utility doctrine.[110]

B. Investment Arbitration Proceedings

1. Eli Lilly's Position

Eli Lilly's claims were based on the general premise that the "promise utility doctrine", as such, applied to their two patents constituted the breach of the obligations imposed on Canada by the NAFTA Investment Chapter.

First of all, Eli Lilly tried to show that the "promise utility doctrine" was a "radically new, additional requirement for patentability."[111] According to Eli Lilly the "promise utility doctrine" required a heightened evidentiary and disclosure standard.[112] Eli Lilly claimed that the doctrine was a novel occurrence in Canadian patent law and that such requirements had not existed at the time the patents at issue were filled.[113]

The doctrine was impermissible both at a domestic law level as well as under international standards, according to Lilly. They went on to explain

---

107 Philip Morris Asia Ltd. v. Australia, PCA Case No. 2012-12 (2011) [herein after: *Philip Morris v. Australia*] available at http://www.italaw.com/cases/851 and Philip Morris Brands Sàrl et al. v. Uruguay, ICSID Case No. ARB/10/7 (2009) (Visited last on Mar. 6, 2018) [herein after: *Philip Morris v. Uruguay*].

108 Vadi, Supra note 51, at 30.

109 Final Award, Supra note 3.

110 See AstraZeneca Canada Inc. v. Apotex Inc., [2017] Supreme Court No. 36654, (Can.), available at: https://scc-csc.lexum.com/scc-csc/scc-csc/en/item/16713/index.do (Visited last on Mar. 6, 2018).

111 *Eli Lilly v. Canada*, Supra note 1, Claimant's Post-hearing Memorial, § 18, available at: http://www.italaw.com/sites/default/files/case-documents/italaw7465.pdf (Visited last on Sept. 14, 2016) [herein after: Claimant's Post-hearing Brief].

112 *Id*, §§ 18-19.

113 *Id*, § 45, § 71.

this claim by taking a comparative approach and contrasting the patent laws of Canada on one side and Mexico and US on the other.[114] The attempt at showing dissonance of Canadian law on utility with the rest of the NAFTA partners, which structure their IP laws according to the same international agreement, was evident. This line of argumentation led to the conclusion that there seems to be a generally accepted standard for utility in jurisdictions across the world. Canada's law was thus portrayed as idiosyncratic.[115]

Having given a characterization of the promise utility doctrine, Lilly used it as a basis to prove breaches of NAFTA IP Chapter provisions. They claimed that the measures undertook by the Canadian courts amounted to both direct and indirect expropriation pursuant to article 1110 as well as the minimum standard of treatment guaranteed by article 1105.[116]

2. Canada's Position

Canada's first defensive arguments suggested that Eli Lilly had failed to construct a proper investment arbitration claim according to NAFTA rules. According to Canada's position, it was manifest that there was no denial of justice. The denial of justice was the only type of action a successful claim can be based on. Without it there could be no breaches of NAFTA articles 1105 and 1110.[117]

The Canadian position then turned to explaining the legitimacy of the standards of utility in their legal system, thus countering Eli Lilly's claims of the "radical new changes" pertaining to the utility requirement.

Canada purported that promises, derived from the patent claims, have been part of Canadian patent before 2005, using the landmark *Consolboard* and *Wellcome* cases as examples of the doctrine's long standing presence in Canadian patent law.[118] The promise doctrine was not only

---

114 *Id*, §§ 136-137.
115 *Id,* § 158.
116 *Id*, §§ 200-1.
117 *Eli Lilly v. Canada*, Supra note 1, Government of Canada Post-hearing Submission, §§ 19-20 available at: http://www.italaw.com/sites/default/files/case-documents/italaw7464.pdf (Visited last on Sept. 14, 2016) [herein after: Respondent's Post-hearing Brief].
118 *Id*, §§ 117-23.

tied to the utility of the patent but also to the over-breadth of protection.[119] Canada went on to explain why the "promise utility doctrine" did not impose a heightened patentability standard. Establishing utility at the moment of filing had always been a requirement of Canadian patent law.[120] Canada likewise claimed that the utility standard offered to pharmaceutical patents was a less stringent requirement than usual, as there was a possibility to claim utility even before it was established.[121] Canada further stated that the interpretation of the utility requirement had not been altered by a new disclosure requirement for claiming utility based on the promise doctrine.[122] Eli Lilly's claims of discrimination of pharmaceutical patents were likewise opposed by Canada. [123] Moreover, Canada pointed that since the alleged changes took place in the mid-2000s, from an international perspective, it had received no complaint regarding the law. This was put into the perspective of the international agreements which Eli Lilly claimed Canada had breached.[124]

Having given its own interpretation of the facts and qualification of the utility requirement in Canadian patent law, Canada rejected both the article 1110 expropriation claim, as well as the 1105, minimum standard of treatment claim.[125]

C. *Legitimate Expectations in Relation to International Intellectual Property Standards*

1. Eli Lilly's Position

Eli Lilly's legitimate expectation claim relied on a number of factors. However, the focus of this thesis is on the relationship of legitimate expectations and international IP treaties, therefore only the arguments related to this relationship will be discussed in detail.

---

119 *Id*, § 131.
120 *Id*, § 139.
121 *Id*, § 148.
122 *Id*, § 151.
123 *Id*, § 222-223.
124 *Id*, § 172.
125 *Id*, § 175.

Eli Lilly claimed that their legitimate violations had been violated, as they had expected that the "promise utility doctrine" would not be inconsistent with Canada's obligations in the NAFTA IP chapter, which in the NAFTA context is the relevant international IP treaty. Eli Lilly claimed that the doctrine was wrong both from a national and an international perspective and that the changes were allegedly, so drastic, that their legitimate expectations had been violated.[126] In order to prove frustration of its legitimate expectations Lilly stated 4 points as to why Canada's utility standard was inconsistent with the NAFTA IP Chapter.

The first point tried to show that the two patents were revoked despite having utility, thus breaching article 1709(1).[127] In order to support its argument Eli Lilly invoked the rules of the VCLT,[128] in particular articles 31 and 32. Eli Lilly held that the promise utility doctrine did not conform to the interpretation rules under article 31 of the VCLT in light of the "text, context, object and purpose, subsequent practice, and relevant rules of international law to interpret the ordinary meaning of the terms 'capable of industrial application' and 'useful.'" Likewise, Eli Lilly claimed that nothing in the interpretative sources[129] pointed to the interpretation that would sustain the "promise utility doctrine".[130]

The second point alleged that the promise utility doctrine discriminates against a field of technology contrary to 1709(7).[131] Eli Lilly stated that there existed a *de facto* discrimination and that their statistical analysis offered as proof, had demonstrated it.[132]

The third point addressed the retrospective application of the doctrine, thus breaching article 1709(8).[133] According to Eli Lilly the doctrine had

---

126 *Eli Lilly v. Canada*, Supra note 1, Claimant's Memorial Index, § 279, available at: http://www.italaw.com/sites/default/files/case-documents/italaw4046.pdf (Visited last on Mar. 6, 2018) [herein after: Claimant's Memorial]; *Eli Lilly v. Canada* Claimant's Reply Memorial, § 364, available at: http://www.italaw.com/sites/default/files/case-documents/italaw4384.pdf (Visited last on Mar. 6, 2018) [herein after: Claimant's Reply], Claimant's Post-hearing Brief, § 280.

127 Claimant's Memorial, Supra note 126, § 186.

128 Vienna Convention on the Law of Treaties, *opened for signature* May 23, 1969, 1155 U.N.T.S. 331.

129 Claimant's Reply, Supra note 126, §§ 283-89.

130 *Id,* § 290.

131 Claimant's Memorial, Supra note 126, § 186.

132 Claimant's Reply, Supra note 126, § 292.

133 Claimant's Memorial, Supra note 126, § 186.

not existed at the moment the patents were filed and they could not have been revoked should the same law still be applicable. [134]

The final point stated that there was a failure to provide adequate protection and enforcement of rights violating article 1701(1).[135] Eli Lilly claimed that by changing the law and retroactively applying it to the two patents, which resulted in their revocation, Canada had essentially denied protection to the two patents.[136]

2. Canada's Position

The basis of Eli Lilly's argument was that the "promise utility doctrine" is inconsistent with the NAFTA Investment Chapter. Canada addresses this first point in the following way:

Canada claimed that it did not breach article 1709(1) as it challenged the way Lilly applied the VCLT, qualifying it "specific" and "extremely restrictive". They accused Eli Lilly of using a "self-serving" interpretation.[137] Canada argued that the proper source for the evaluation of patent law should be domestic law. Patent law is territorial and there are no international definitions for concepts such as utility.[138] Furthermore Canada contended that had the parties wanted to establish a precise meaning of "useful" or "capable of industrial application" they would have provided a definition.[139] Turning to the application of VCLT article 31(1)(c), Canada denied the relevance of the PCT as the relevant rule of law and highlighted the TRIPS which likewise did not provide a precise meaning for the patentability requirements.[140] Lastly, Canada rejected the article 32 argument by claiming that the failure of the SPLT and the SPC survey did not

---

134 Claimant's Reply, Supra note 126, §§ 301-2.
135 Claimant's Memorial, Supra note 126, § 186.
136 Claimant's Reply, Supra note 126, § 306.
137 *Eli Lilly v. Canada*, Government of Canada Rejoinder Memorial, § 139, available at: http://www.italaw.com/sites/default/files/case-documents/ITA%20LAW %207014.pdf (Visited last on Mar. 6, 2018) [herein after: Respondent's Rejoinder Memorial].
138 *Id*, § 151.
139 *Id*, § 169.
140 *Id*, §§ 178-81.

provide any kind of restrictive standardization of the utility requirement.[141]

Canada rejected Eli Lilly's violation claim of 1709(7) by stating that Eli
Lilly's argument was based on a flawed interpretation of statistics. Canada
thus held that there was no *de facto* discrimination against pharmaceutical
patents.[142]

Canada further rejected Lilly's claims in relation to article 1709(8). It
states that the law had not been applied retroactively, rather jurisprudence
had developed over time. Canada stated that evolving legal standards applied to the patent during the whole patent term.[143]

Canada likewise rejected the claim related to article 1701(1). It stated
that its law offered a comprehensive system of IP protection by giving
substantive protection to IPRs and providing an enforcement mechanism
as well. This was contrary to Lilly's arguments of the system being inef-
fective. Canada supported the defense with statistical proof.[144]

With this line of argumentation Canada rejected the inconsistency of its
law with the NAFTA IP Chapter. However, Canada likewise held that
even if there had been inconsistencies, they could not have amounted to a
breach of article 1105. This view was based on the FTC's Note[145] which
stated that a breach of another international treaty does not amount to a
breach of article 1105.[146]

However finally, the complex exchange of argumentation was never really addressed by the Tribunal. The Tribunal ruled that the law as applied
to the promise utility doctrine did not constitute a violation of either article
1105 and 1110 of the NAFTA. Moreover, it stated that that there was no
arbitrary or discriminatory measure that can infringe either of the articles.[147] In that regard the Tribunal was satisfied with its findings, seeing
no need to address further arguments, including the ones regarding legitimate expectations and the NAFTA IP Chapter. However, the arguments

---

141 *Id*, §§ 183-84.
142 *Id*, §§ 190-203.
143 *Id*, § 207.
144 *Id*, § 134-137.
145 Notes of Interpretation of Certain Chapter Eleven Provisions (Free Trade Com-
     mission, July 31, 2001), available at http://www.international.gc.ca (Visited last
     on Mar. 6, 2018) [herein after: FTC's Note].
146 Respondent's Rejoinder Memorial, Supra note 137, § 295.
147 Final Award, Supra note 3, § 442.

still have value as it is possible that similar arguments might be proposed in future investment arbitration cases.

IV. "Promise Utility Doctrine"

A. Canadian Law and Courts

Canada has a mixed legal tradition which is reflected on the state of the law today. The first influx of European law came with the French settlers in the 16th century who brought along the civil law tradition.[148] After the victory of the English in the colonial wars in the mid-18th century they started implementing their own legal practices. During the centuries, as Canada was slowly gaining more independence, the judicial and legal links with the English crown were equally being severed.[149] Until 1949 the final appeals court of Canada was an English court — the Judicial Committee of the Privy Council.[150] Nowadays Canada has a fully independent legal system.

The Canadian court system consists of two parts – the main court system and the federal court system. At the top of both systems stands the Supreme Court of Canada. The main court system is territory or province based. The courts in this system can only hear issues arising out of provincial or territorial law.[151] The federal court system adjudicates matters emanating from federal law. The federal courts are therefore in charge of hearing many issues regarding IP.[152] The Patent Act, being a federal act, is subject to the scrutiny of Canadian Federal Courts.

---

148 Jessi J. Horner, Canadian Law and the Canadian Legal System, 41-3 (2007).
149 *Id,* at 46-7.
150 *Id,* at 47.
151 *Id,* at 242-43.
152 *Id,* at 243-44.

B. Patent Law in Canada

1. Historical Developments

Canadian patent laws are based on the Canadian Patent Act. The right of the Federal government to create such a statute stems from the Constitution Act which vests the power of creating legislation in relation to "[p]atents of inventions and discoveries."[153] The first federal Patent Act was created in 1869,[154] influenced by its two predecessors – the Lower Canada Patent Act of 1823 and the Upper Canada Patent Act of 1826. These acts were in turn significantly influenced by two legal traditions – the English common law legal tradition with the rules coming from the Statute of Monopolies (British patent law was not codified at the time of the two Canadian patent acts) and the United States legal tradition with its codified Patent Act of 1793.[155] The traces of these traditions can be seen in contemporary Canadian patent law. Although codified in the Canadian Patent Act, patent law is still molded by common law traditions.

2. Pharmaceutical Patents in Canada

It is often stated that patent protection is essential for the survival and development of the pharmaceutical industry.[156] Canada is nowadays offering patent protection to pharmaceuticals. However, these rules are of a fairly recent nature. Since the initial Patent Act was enacted in 1869 it has undergone many changes and amendments which included the changes in the temporal length of patent protection,[157] rules addressing chemical and medical inventions,[158] compulsory licensing rules[159] and in particular spe-

---

153 Constitution Act, 1867, § 91(22), 30 & 31 Vict. Ch. 3 (U. K.), *as reprinted in* R.S.C., No. 5 (Appendix 1985).
154 ELIZABETH F. JUDGE & DANIEL J. GERVAIS, INTELLECTUAL PROPERTY: THE LAW IN CANADA, 2nd ed., 645 (2011).
155 STEPHEN J. PERRY & T. ANDREW CURRIER, CANADIAN PATENT LAW, 2nd ed., 24-5 (2014)
156 Juan Bacalski, MEXICO'S PHARMACEUTICAL PATENT DILEMMA AND THE LESSONS OF INDIA, 23 Ariz. J. Int'l & Comp. Law, 717, 717 (2006).
157 1883, 1886, 1892, 1935, 1989. Perry & Currier, Supra note 150, at 31-7.
158 1923. *Id,* at 32.
159 1903, 1906, 1923. *Id.*

cific rules regarding compulsory licensing of pharmaceuticals.[160] Compulsory licenses were commonly granted in order to produce medicine which were patent protected and would normally constitute patent infringement.[161] The last rule was introduced as a policy measure to ensure that "Canadian consumers have access to reasonably priced medicines."[162] This sparked the rise of the Canadian generic industry.[163] This provision was unsurprisingly unpopular with the international pharmaceutical companies. Through lobbying efforts, they pushed for a patent law reform which eventually resulted in the Patent Act of 1989, which, with minor amendments from 1996, stands as it is today. In 1993 Canada, preparing the compliance of its laws with the coming of the NAFTA and the TRIPS, abandoned its compulsory licensing scheme.[164]

3. Patent Law Basic Principles

Patents are granted for inventions. According to the Canadian Patent Act an invention "means any new and useful art, process, machine, manufacture or composition of matter, or any new and useful improvement in any art, process, machine, manufacture or composition of matter;"[165] In order for the inventor to acquire the rights granted by the Patent Act for its invention, he or she must disclose the details of the invention in full. After the patent protection expires, the patent falls into the public domain and the public is free to use the invention.[166] In order to acquire the patent rights a patent must be granted first. The granting of a patent is done through a registration process. During this process four formal requirements must be met: The invention must be fall under the protectable subject matter, it must be new, inventive and useful.[167]

---

160 1969. *Id,* at 34-5.
161 Adam Falconi, CETA: An Opportunity to Fix Canada's Broken Pharmaceutical Patent Linkage System, 27 I.P.J., 325, 330 (2015).
162 Perry & Currier, Supra note 155, at 25.
163 Falconi, Supra note 161, at 330.
164 *Id at* 330-31.
165 Patent Act, § 2, R.S.C., c. P-4 (Can.).
166 Martin P.J. Kratz, Q.C., Canada's Intellectual Property Law in a Nutshell, 2nd ed., 202 (2010).
167 *Id,* at 223.

a) Protectable Subject Matter

The protectable subject matter is the preliminary requirement for a grant of a patent. A patent can only be granted if the nature of the invention is recognized by the Patent act[168], the matter is not excluded under its statutory requirements and if it avoids the court created exemptions.[169] Without the invention fulfilling this precondition, the analysis of patentability is redundant. The invention might satisfy the rest of the requirements, however if it is by its nature excluded from patenting, the patent will not be granted.

b) Patentability Requirements

Having established that the invention falls under the patentable subject matter, the invention needs to be analyzed under the remaining three patentability requirements – novelty, obviousness and utility.

(1) Novelty

The novelty requirement is derived from section 2 of the Patent act.[170] If the invention is not novel the patent application will be rejected.[171] The Supreme Court of Canada acknowledged that novelty is at the heart of the patent bargain. "If the public has been put into possession of the claimed invention by whatever means, it does not have to pay the price of monopoly to get it again."[172]

(2) Non-Obviousness

Non-Obviousness is a patentability requirement which ensures that the advances made by an invention are not miniscule and that they possess "in-

---

168 Patent Act, Supra note 165, § 2.
169 Perry & Currier, Supra note 155, at 90.
170 Patent Act, Supra note 165, § 2.
171 *Id.*
172 Perry & Currier, Supra note 155, at 178.

ventive merit." Non-obviousness was not an express statutory category prior to the act of 1989. However, since then its statutory basis is to be found in article 28.3. of the Patent Act. The assessment of non-obviousness is assumed from the perspective of the person skilled in the art and his or hers assessment of the prior art.[173]

(3) Utility

For a patent to be granted the invention must be useful. The way this patentability requirement is defined and what is its scope, is at the core of the *Eli Lilly* case. The utility requirement has been present in statutory Canadian patent law since the early patent statutes.[174] However in comparison with other terms coming from section 2 of the patent Act, utility has received far less judicial elaboration.[175] The term itself had no fixed meaning and it evolved over time. As far as 1841 utility was held by the Canadian courts to be "an apparatus that would answer some beneficial purpose."[176] In 1940 a Canadian court stated: "An invention to be patentable must confer on the public a benefit. Utility as predicated of inventions, means industrial value. No patent can be granted for a worthless art or arrangement."[177] More recently and relevant for the *Eli Lilly* case is the definition the Supreme Court of Canada used in *Consolboard* case. Justice Dickson used the concept of "not useful" in the context of patent law found in Halsbury's Laws of England (3rd ed.) He stated: "It means that the invention will not work, either in the sense it will not operate at all, or more broadly, that it will not do what the specification promises that it will do."[178] This definition created a fork like approach to determining the utility of a patent. Not only is the total absence of utility excluded from satisfying the utility requirement, rather the discord of the stated utility and the established utility will hold the invention not useful. The definition introduced the term "promise" which is the key term in determining the second fork approach. This approach was confirmed in the case of *Eli Lilly v.*

---

173 Kratz, Supra note 166, at 228-9
174 Perry & Currier, Supra note 155, at 129.
175 *Id,* at 130.
176 *Id,* at 131.
177 *Id.*
178 *Id.*

Novopharm,[179] which is one of the two relevant cases for the investment arbitration. "The general principle is that, as of the relevant date (the date of filing), there must have been either demonstration of utility of the invention or a sound prediction of the utility. Evidence beyond that set out in the specification can, and normally will, be necessary." The court proceeded to elaborate on the relationship of utility and its promise: "Where the specification does not promise a specific result, no particular level of utility is required; a 'mere scintilla' of utility will suffice. However, where the specification sets out an explicit 'promise,' utility will be measured against that promise: *Consolboard; Pfizer Canada Inc. v. Canada (Minister of Health),* [2009] 1 F.C.R. 253, 2008 FCA 108 (*Rambaxy*). The question is whether the invention does what the patent promises it will do."[180]

(a) Demonstrated Utility

The demonstrated utility does not relate to any valuation of its intended use or any attributed value to it. The only referential point according to the Canadian Patent Act is that the patent will do what has been described and claimed in the patent.[181] Moreover there is no requirement for the patentee to establish utility in the patent. Utility is then assumed from the wording of the patent. Nevertheless, when certain improvements are directly prescribed in the patent, it is expected that these improvements materialize upon the patent's deployment or construction. If they do not materialize the patent can be found invalid.[182] An example stated by professors Perry and Currier in their book nicely illustrates this difference. A mechanical invention patent that plainly instructs how to build the invention without any prescribed promises is found useful if a person skilled in the art follows the instruction and builds the invention. However, in a pharmaceutical selection patent the invention is found in the choice of a compound from a group of compounds. A direct promise is necessary in such cases, as the promise lies in the explanation (description) of the choice of that

---

179 *Eli Lilly v. Novopharm*, Supra note 96.
180 Perry & Currier, Supra note 155, at 131.
181 *Id,* at 133.
182 *Id,* at 134.

particular compound.[183] Different types of patents, even though *de jure* subject to the exact same requirement of utility, in practice apply the requirement differently. A one-size-fits-all approach is not applicable here. However, utility must be demonstrated at the moment of patent application. If not demonstrated the utility can be soundly predicted.[184]

(b) Sound Prediction Doctrine

As opposed to the demonstration of utility at the moment of patent filing, Canadian patent law allows another possibility for the patentee to satisfy the utility requirement. When the patentee is unable to demonstrate utility at the appropriate date a patent may be granted on the basis of a sound prediction of utility.[185] The principal reason behind this doctrine was stated in the *Apotex v. Wellcome*[186] case. "The doctrine of 'sound prediction' balances the public interest in early disclosure of new and useful inventions, even before their utility has been verified by tests (which is the case of pharmaceutical products may take years) and the public interest in avoiding cluttering the public domain with useless patents, and granting monopoly rights in exchange for misinformation."[187] The *Apotex v. Wellcome* case is not only relevant for formulating the justification of the sound prediction doctrine but also for the creation of the three-element test by the Canadian courts. In order to determine if there are grounds for a sound prediction of utility the court must determine "1) [a] factual basis for the prediction; 2) the inventor's articulable and 'sound' line of reasoning, at the date of the patent application, from which the desired result can be inferred from the factual basis; and 3) proper disclosure." As such the sound prediction is a matter of fact.[188]

---

183 *Id,* at 134.
184 Judge & Gervais, Supra note 154, at 728.
185 *Id,* at 727-28.
186 Apotex Inc. v. Wellcome Foundation Ltd., [2002] 4 SCR 153, 2002 SCC 77 (Can.) [herein after: Apotex v. Wellcome].
187 *Id,* at 155.
188 Judge & Gervais, Supra note 154. at 728.

(3) Promise of a Patent

Another constituent part of the utility requirement which is closely related to the sound prediction is the patent promise. The promise of a patent means that the invention in the patent will achieve what has been written in the claims and description. The court is the one responsible for interpreting and ascertaining what the promise of a patent actually is. However, there is no obligation for the inventor to disclose the promise of utility, except "where a promised utility is at the core of the novelty of the invention." This rule is particularly important for pharmaceutical patents as sometimes the utility of the pharmaceutical patent cannot be clearly determined at the moment of patenting.[189]

The sound prediction doctrine and the promise of the patent doctrine joined together are what in the *Eli Lilly v. Canada* case is called the "promise utility doctrine." In essence this doctrine posits that when it is not possible for the utility of the patent to be demonstrated at the moment of the filing, the patent applicant can "promise" such utility. However, he or she must provide ample evidence that indicate the possibility that the utility will be proved in the future.

C. Compliance of Doctrine with International Intellectual Property Standards

The approach taken by Lilly to establish violations of NAFTA articles 1110 and 1105 heavily relies on the claim that the "promise utility doctrine" is inconsistent with international IP norms. So, is the promise utility doctrine really inconsistent with international IP standards?

The concepts of "novelty", "inventive step" or "non-obviousness" and "industrial application" or "utility" have been for a long time a matter of debate in domestic legal systems and they have been put under the test of litigation many times.[190] And even though there seems to be a level of proximity of all of the concepts, their interpretation still remains different

---

189 Perry & Currier, Supra note 155, at 141-43.
190 Kathleen Liddell & Michael Waibel, FAIR AND EQUITABLE TREATMENT AND JUDICIAL PATENT DECISIONS, 19 J. Int'l Econ. L., 145, 150 (2016).

across jurisdictions.[191] However patent law has historically been diverse.[192] From an international perspective the situation is quite the opposite. The TRIPS is an agreement that leaves a number of concepts undefined or defined broadly[193] and states have been using this opportunity to curtail the laws according to their domestic policy goals. Such laws often find opposition. The common argument is that they do not comply with the obligations set out in the TRIPS. Perhaps the most well-known case is the *Novartis* case and the section 3(d) of the Indian Patent Act.[194] The section limits the patentability of new forms of already known substances. Novartis lost one of its pharmaceutical patents according to the provision. Consequently, it brought the case before the Indian courts, where one of the claims was that the particular provision is inconsistent with the TRIPS. The Indian court declined jurisdiction over the claim. The question of consistency of the particular provision was never brought before the WTO dispute settlement mechanism. Therefore, the consistency of the norm with the TRIPS is implied and all considerations remain in the realm of academic debate.[195] As such the provision still stands today. This does not however mean that the provision is still present in law because it was not challenged despite its perceived illegality. There are arguments that point to its possible compliance with the TRIPS. WTO allows a level of differentiation for specific areas, whose subject matter are in themselves specific.[196] Therefore this provision can be justified as falling under the allowed

---

191 Even authors who argue for uniformity of the concepts recognize that they are not identical in different jurisdictions – "remarkably similar". See, Jay Erstling, Amy M. Samela & Justin N. Woo, *Usefulness Varies by Country: The Utility Requirement of Patent Law in the United States, Europe and Canada*, Faculty Scholarship Paper 3(1) Cybaris, 1, 12 (2012).

192 *The U.S. Expansion of Patentable Subject Matter: Creating a Competitive Advantage for Foreign Multinational Companies?*, 18 B.U. Int'l L.J., 111, 112 (2000)

193 Liddell & Waibel, Supra note 190, at 150.

194 The Patents (Amendment) Act, § 3(d), No. 15 of 2005, India Code (2005) [herein after: Indian Patent Act].

195 Henning Grosse Ruse-Khan & Roberto Romandini, PATENTABILITY OF PHARMACEUTICAL INVENTIONS UNDER TRIPS, DOMESTIC COURT PRACTICE AS A TEST FOR INTERNATIONAL POLICY SPACE, (Max Planck Institute for Innovation and Competition Research Paper Ser., Paper No. 16-02, 2016), 1, 30 http://papers.ssrn.com/sol3/papers.cfm?abstract_id=2736224 (Visited last on Mar. 6, 2018).

196 Cynthia M. Ho, SHOULD ALL DRUGS BE PATENTABLE?: A COMPARATIVE PERSPECTIVE, 17 Vand. J. Ent. & Tech. L., 295, 340 (2015).

differentiation and not under forbidden discrimination. However, until decided by the competent adjudicatory body, the provision's consistency should be presumed.

A similar approach can be applied to the "promise utility doctrine". The interpretation of the NAFTA is in the jurisdiction of the NAFTA state to state dispute settlement[197] under the Institutional Arrangements and Dispute Settlement Procedures Chapter or the FTC. The doctrine has been in existence for some time and the NAFTA parties have had the chance to challenge the existence and the use of the doctrine, as incompatible with NAFTA IP Chapter rules. However, until now no challenge of the sort had been logged. This reason for this can be that other NAFTA member states have similar doctrines in their own patent laws.[198]

The fact that both dispute resolution options under the TRIPS and the NAFTA are left to challenge at the discretion of the states, private parties must seek recourse in other fora. A worldwide corporate law firm, Jones Day, has in an open publication advised pharmaceutical patent holders to challenge such measure in investment arbitration. A way to do that is to adapt their claims so that the measures taken by the state can be qualified as violations of the FET standard and legitimate expectations.[199]

---

197 One of the most common proceedings of state to state arbitration is to obtain an interpretation of the treaty. See, Nathalie Bernasconi-Osterwalder, STATE-STATE DISPUTE SETTLEMENT IN INVESTMENT TREATIES, (IISD Best Practice Ser. 2014), 1, 8. https://www.iisd.org/sites/default/files/publications/best-practices-state-state-dispute-settlement-investment-treaties.pdf (Visited last on Mar. 6, 2018).

198 Norman Siebrasse, HGS v. LILLY: HOW SOON IS TOO SOON TO PATENT?, 24 I. P. J., 41, 45 (2011).

199 *Treaty Protection for Global Patents: A Response to a Growing Problem for Multinational Pharmaceutical Companies*, Jones Day Publications (2012) available at: http://www.jonesday.com/treaty_protection/ (Visited last on Mar. 6, 2018).

V. Fair and Equitable Treatment Standard and Legitimate Expectations

The FET standard and legitimate expectations are inherently linked. This connection does not have a standardized form but the majority of investment Tribunals treat these two concepts as closely related. In such a manner they will be observed in this thesis.

A. Fair and Equitable Treatment Standard

1. General Characteristics

Most IIAs contain a clause that provides for the standard of protection known as FET. The German model BIT 2008[200], for example, contains the following provision: "Each contracting State shall in its territory in every case accord investments by investors of the other Contracting State fair and equitable treatment as well as full protection under this Treaty."[201] The FET standard is the most called upon standard of protection in investment arbitration and FET claims are deemed highly successful. Despite the standard's presence in IIAs, a surge of FET claims has been seen only since the *Metalclad* v. *Mexico* case.[202]

Historically the FET standard is rooted in the US treaties on Friendship, Commerce and Navigation.[203] Its modern manifestation was given for the first time in the Havana Charter for International Trade Organizations in 1948, where the term "just and equitable treatment" was used. Even though the Treaty which remained only a draft and which was never, in fact envisaged as an investment treaty, ensured FET its first prominent

---

200 German Model Treaty-2008, Treaty between the Federal Republic of Germany and (empty space) concerning the Encouragement and Reciprocal Protection of Investments, available at: http://investmentpolicyhub.unctad.org/Download/TreatyFile/2865 (Visited last on Mar. 6, 2018) [herein after: German Model BIT].
201 *Id*, art. 2(2).
202 Rudolf Dolzer & Christoph Schreuer, Principles of International Investment Law, 1st ed., 119, (2008).
203 *Id*, at 120.

role.[204] Today FET protection is a ubiquitous standard, although it was not always present in IIAs. Over time, and especially since the conclusion of the first modern BIT between Germany and Pakistan[205], FET started to appear more regularly in IIAs.[206]

The purpose of the FET standard is to fill the gaps left by the rules on expropriation, which addresses the direct or indirect taking of property.[207] This means that an investor can sometimes count on the protection through this standard independently of the Tribunal's decision on expropriation.[208] Therefore FET protects the investor from different kinds of unfair situations.[209] The FET standard is applied as a "yardstick for the conduct of the national legislator, of domestic administrations, and of domestic courts."[210] Furthermore FET is an absolute standard. It applies to investments without regard to the State's treatment of other entities and investments.[211] It is as such a rule of international law and it cannot be based on domestic laws of the state. Therefore, violations of FET can be found even if there seems to be no breach of the national treatment obligation.[212]

However, the precise source of FET as a standard in international law is not entirely clear. It is generally accepted that FET is a part of customary international law but that is where the consensus stops.[213] Some consider the standard to be related to the customary international law standard for the treatment of aliens, as it was originally connected to it in the draft of

---

204 LUKAS VANHONNAEKER, INTELLECTUAL PROPERTY RIGHTS AS FOREIGN DIRECT INVESTMENTS: FROM COLLISION TO COLLABORATION, 101 (2015).
205 Germany – Pakistan BIT, Supra note 50.
206 RONALD KLÄGER, 'FAIR AND EQUITABLE TREATMENT' IN INTERNATIONAL INVESTMENT LAW, 10 (2011).
207 Dolzer & Schreuer, Supra note 202, at 122.
208 Jean Kalicki & Suzana Medeiros, FAIR, EQUITABLE AND AMBIGUOUS: WHAT IS THE FAIR AND EQUITABLE TREATMENT IN INTERNATIONAL INVESTMENT LAW?, 22 (1) ICSID Rev. Foreign Invs't L. J., 24, 25 (2007).
209 *Fair and Equitable Treatment,* UNCTAD Series On Issues In International Investment Agreements II, 6-7 (2012) [herein after: FET UNCTAD].
210 STEPHAN W. SCHILL, THE MULITILATERIZATION OF INTERNATIONAL INVESTMENT LAW, 79 (2009).
211 FET UNCTAD, Supra note 209, at 6.
212 Dolzer & Schreuer, Supra note 202, at 123.
213 Jacob Stone, ARBITRARINESS, THE FAIR AND EQUITABLE TREATMENT STANDARD, AND THE INTERNATIONAL LAW OF INVESTMENT, 25(1) L.J.I.L. 77, 78 (2012).

the OECD convention.[214] Some however view the standard as a standalone standard without express connection to other rules of international law.[215] The qualification of the FET standard is furthermore important for its substantive content. The language of the FET provisions is often broad and vague. The arbitral Tribunals are therefore the ones who give meaning to such broadly defined provisions[216]. For that reason, the FET standard has been criticized for lacking predictability and being susceptible to expansive interpretation.[217]

However, there are some recurring concepts that Tribunals regularly consider when deciding on the violations of the standard. According to some authors five distinct points could be put under the chapeau of the FET standard:

1. Legitimate expectations – The acts or promises of the state give rise to legitimate expectations of the investor.
2. Non-discrimination – Investors are protected from discriminatory acts of the state.
3. Fair procedure – The investor is guaranteed regular access and recourse through administrative and judicial mechanisms.
4. Transparency – The investor is afforded access to clear information in regards to the domestic legal framework and procedures.
5. Proportionality – This notion requires the Tribunal to balance the interest of the investor and the state in light of the measure taken that might have resulted in the violation of the FET standard.[218]

---

214 OECD, The Multilateral Agreement on Investment Draft Consolidated Text, § IV, art. 1, DAFFE/MAI(98)7/REV1 (1998) available at: http://www1.oecd.org/daf/mai/pdf/ng/ng987r1e.pdf (Visited last on Mar. 6, 2018).

215 FET UNCTAD, Supra note 209, at 7-8.

216 The Tribunal made an interpretative reference to the objectives of the treaty and found that transparency should be a part of the FET standard. Metalclad Corp. v. Mexico Award, §§ 75-76, ICSID Case No. ARB(AF)/97/1 (2001)[herein after: *Metalclad v. Mexico*].

217 FET UNCTAD, Supra note 209, at 6-7.

218 Kläger, Supra note 206, at 10.

2. The Fair and Equitable Treatment Standard under NAFTA

NAFTA jurisprudence on the FET standard is somewhat specific. The provision which provides fair and equitable treatment is located under article 1105(1):

> "Each Party shall accord to investments of investors of another Party treatment in accordance with international law, including fair and equitable treatment and full protection and security."

The standard only reached a degree of uniformity after the FTC issued its seminal Note[219]. Prior to the FTC's Note *Metalclad v. Mexico* was the first award to elaborate on the standard. The follow up Tribunals after *Metalclad* v. Mexico did not however accept the same interpretative discourse.

a) Metalclad v. Mexico

In *Metalclad v. Mexico* the investor, relying on the government of Mexico's permit to run its business, was later denied the opportunity to do so by the municipality.[220] Therefore the two branches of the same government presented conflicting messages and behavior to the investor, resulting in its inability to continue the business. The Tribunal found that the violation of FET occurred in the following manner:

> "Mexico failed to ensure a transparent and predictable framework for Metalclad's business planning and investment. The totality of these circumstances demonstrates a lack of orderly process and timely disposition in relation to an investor of a Party acting in the expectation that it would be treated fairly and justly in accordance with the NAFTA."[221]

---

219 FTC's Note, Supra note 145.
220 *Metalclad v. Mexico,* Supra note 216, §§ 47-50.
221 Id, § 99.

b) S. D. Myers v. Canada[222]

Another NAFTA investment Tribunal found a violation of FET in the *S. D. Myers* case. The article 1105 issue was whether the violation of the national treatment standard directly indicates the violation of FET. The Tribunal left room for a possibility that a breach of the national treatment does not directly lead to a violation of FET.[223] However, what was perhaps more interesting is the definition the Tribunal provided for the threshold needed to reach a violation of FET. The Tribunal stated:

> "Article 1105(1) expresses an overall concept. The words of the article must be read as a whole. The phrases *...fair and equitable treatment...* and *...full protection and security...* cannot be read in isolation. They must be read in conjunction with the introductory phrase *...treatment in accordance with international law.*"[224]

The Tribunal considered that a breach of article 1105 occurs only when it is shown that an investor has been treated in such "an unjust or arbitrary manner that the treatment rises to the level that is unacceptable from the international perspective. That determination must be made in the light of the high measure of deference that international law generally extends to the right of domestic authorities to regulate matters within their own borders. The determination must also take into account any specific rules of international law that are applicable to the case."[225]

The departure from the *Metalclad* case was evident. The FET standard was treated in a more abstract manner and more importantly it recognized two distinct points – the breach of the standard is connected to the state's international law obligations and the deference to national law in light of the state's right to regulate.

---

222 S.D. Myers, Inc. v. Canada Partial Award (2004), available at: http://www.italaw.com/sites/default/files/case-documents/ita0747.pdf (Visited last on Mar. 6, 2018) [herein after *S.D. Myers v. Canada*].

223 *Id,* § 266.

224 *Id*, § 262.

225 Id, § 263.

c) Pope & Talbot v. Canada[226]

Another prominent case, after which the FTC's Note was eventually issued, was the *Pope & Talbot* case. The Tribunal took on an "additive" approach, thus holding that the FET standard contained in 1105(1) goes beyond the minimum standard of treatment of aliens found in international customary law. The Tribunal stated:

> "Accordingly, the Tribunal interprets Article 1105 to require that covered investors and investments receive the elements of the fairness benefits under ordinary standards applied in the NAFTA countries without any threshold limitation that the conduct complained be of 'egregious,' 'outrageous,' or 'shocking,' or otherwise extraordinary."[227]

The interpretation gave way for an open-ended direction in the development of jurisprudence on the FET standard. Therefore, the FTC's Note can be seen as a pre-emptive move to defer future Tribunals from further widening the FET standard. The FTC's interpretative Note stated:

> "The concepts of 'fair and equitable treatment' and 'full protection and security' do not require treatment in addition to or beyond that which is required by the customary international law minimum standard of treatment of aliens."[228]

A clear signal was sent. The Note did not address just one issue. More interpretative guidance was given in the Note. Under article B(3) of the Note the following is pronounced:

> "A determination that there has been a breach of another provision of the NAFTA, or of a separate international agreement, does not establish that there has been a breach of Article 1105(1)."[229]

This interpretative rule prohibited a direct causal link between breaches of international law and the FET standard. Therefore, when a breach of international or other NAFTA obligation is found, it should be treated from a case specific viewpoint. What comes from this is that an investor cannot solely rely on proving the breach of the international legal norm, rather it

---

226 *Pope & Talbot Inc. v. Canada*, UNCITRAL,Award on the Merits of Phase II, (2001), available at: http://www.italaw.com/sites/default/files/case-documents/ ita0678.pdf (Visited last on Mar. 6, 2018) [herein after: *Pope & Talbot v. Canada*].

227 *Id*, § 118.

228 FTC's Note, Supra note 145, art. B(2).

229 *Id*, art. B(3).

needs to be placed into context of the conduct amounting to the breach of the possible FET standard.

d) Mondev v. USA[230]

The first case after the FTC's Note was the *Mondev v. USA* case. It was the first time a NAFTA investment Tribunal applied the Note in practice. The Tribunal accepted the connection to the international law standard. However, it firstly rejected the standard set in the *Neer* case as currently applicable.[231] The Tribunal made a further clarification that the standard evolves over time and that the Note's language points to the contemporary standard of customary international law. The Tribunal stated:

"But in its view, there can be no doubt that, by interpreting Article 1105(1) to prescribe the customary international law minimum standard of treatment of aliens as the minimum standard of treatment to be afforded to investments of investors of another Party under NAFTA, the term 'customary international law' refers to customary international law as it stood no earlier than the time at which NAFTA came into force. It is not limited to the international law of the 19th century or even of the first half of the 20th century, although decisions from that period remain relevant. In holding that Article 1105(1) refers to customary international law, the FTC interpretations incorporate current international law, whose content is shaped by the conclusion of more than two thousand bilateral investment treaties and many treaties of friendship and commerce."[232]

After *Mondev v. USA* the NAFTA investment Tribunals decided on a number of cases where the designated interpretation of article 1105(1) was used. However even this circumscribed version of article 1105 left room for various application of the standard, owing to the specific factual situation of the cases.

---

230 Mondev I'ntl Ltd. v. USA, ICSID (Additional Facility) Award, Case No. ARB(AF)/99/2 (2002), available at: http://www.italaw.com/sites/default/files/case-documents/ita1076.pdf (Visited last on Mar. 6, 2018) [herein after: *Mondev v. USA*].
231 *Id*, § 116.
232 *Id*, § 125.

e) Waste Management v. Mexico[233]

Despite the Note's limiting effect NAFTA's FET jurisprudence kept on evolving even after *Mondev v. USA*. In the *Waste Management v. Mexico* the Tribunal made way to what was to become the basis for legitimate expectations, although a clear distinction was not made at the time. The Tribunal stated:

> "[T]hat the minimum standard of treatment of fair and equitable treatment is infringed by conduct attributable to the State and harmful to the claimant if the conduct is arbitrary, grossly unfair, unjust or idiosyncratic, is discriminatory and exposes the claimant to sectional or racial prejudice, or involves a lack of due process leading to an outcome which offends judicial propriety—as might be the case with a manifest failure of natural justice in judicial proceedings or a complete lack of transparency and candor in an administrative process. In applying this standard it is relevant that the treatment is in breach of representations made by the host State which were reasonably relied on by the claimant."[234]

The FET standard definition given by the *Waste Management* Tribunal relied primarily on the denial of justice and transparency. However, the last sentence introduced, very clearly, the concept of legitimate expectations as a part of the FET standard. The jurisprudential influence of *Metalclad v. Mexico* is likewise evident. Its reference to the establishment of a transparent and predictable legal system very well corresponded with the concept of legitimate expectation.

B. Legitimate Expectations

1. General Characteristics

The root of the concept of legitimate relates to the "phenomenon of 'change'". An investment, whatever form it assumes, usually persists for a prolonged period of time. It is very rarely an instantaneous and "one-off" business act. During this time the investment might be affected by adverse

---

233 Waste Management Inc. v. Mexico, ICSID (Additional Facility) Award, Case No. ARB(AF)/00/3 (2004), available at: http://www.italaw.com/sites/default/files/case-documents/ita0900.pdf (Visited last on Mar. 6, 2018) [herein after: *Waste Management v. Mexico*].

234 *Id*, § 98.

changes coming from different sources. Some are a result of economic factors or technological development. However, some acts of the state like regulatory measures and the implementation of a law can affect investments as well. The second type of situation is the one legitimate expectations address.[235] The core notion of legitimate expectations is that an investor is able to rely on certain state acts when making its investment decisions. However not all expectations are considered protectable under international investment law.[236]

The concept of legitimate expectations is usually accepted as falling under the chapeau of the FET standard, which is on the one hand clearly worded in IIAs. On the other hand, there rarely seems to be clear wording in FET provisions pointing to the protection of legitimate expectations.[237] So how exactly does a concept like legitimate expectations persist in investment arbitration jurisprudence? As some authors suggest legitimate expectations can be viewed as a general principle of law.[238] General principles of law are usually supplementary means of interpretation used for gap filling of provisions[239] or as means to resolve conflicts between overlapping provisions and rules.[240] Nevertheless in establishing the link one needs to look to existing legal systems where legitimate expectations are firmly grounded. Therefore, some authors suggest looking at municipal law[241] and public law[242] in different jurisdictions as possible sources. By taking the core of the concept, based on the recurring characteristic of the principle in the observed jurisdictions, which would be "suited for the international environment", could provide a source to the principle.[243] From the perspective of legal theory this line of reasoning has some standing. In

---

235 FET UNCTAD, Supra note 209, at 63-64.
236 Christoph Schreuer & Ursula Kriebaum, AT WHAT TIME MUST LEGITIMATE EXPECTATIONS EXIST? in A Liber Amicorum: Thomas Wälde - Law Beyond Conventional Thought, 265, 265 (Jacques Werner & Arif Hyder Ali 1st ed. 2009).
237 Michele Potesta, LEGITIMATE EXPECTATIONS IN INVESTMENT TREATY LAW: UNDERSTANDING THE ROOTS AND THE LIMITS OF A CONTROVERSIAL CONCEPT, 28(1) ICSID - For. Inv. L.J., 88, 90 (2013).
238 Elizabeth Snodgrass, PROTECTING INVESTOR'S LEGITIMATE EXPECTATIONS: RECOGNIZING AND DELIMITING THE GENERAL PRINCIPLE, 21(1) ICSID - For. Inv. L.J., 1, 11 (2006).
239 *Id,* at 13.
240 *Id,* at 19.
241 *Id,* at 18.
242 *Id,* at 21.
243 *Id,* at 23.

practice though, investment Tribunals do not apply this approach. According to some authors there seems to be little regard for real state practice.[244] Likewise the Tribunals are likely to look at previous decisions of other Tribunals, thus effectively creating a rule of precedent in international investment arbitration.[245]

The substantive content of legitimate expectations varies, although there seems to be a general understanding of which notions they carry. In essence the investor is able to base its expectations on certain conditions attributable to the state provided at the time of the investment. The conditions cannot be established on a unilateral basis, they must exist in law and be enforceable by it. If the state has failed to respect its promises it is required to compensate the investor expect in cases of state necessity. The investor cannot disregard parameters such as industry patterns and business risk when creating its expectations.[246]

The question to be asked here is – what type of condition can the investor rely on and which expectations can be legitimate? Three distinct approaches can be found.

a) Legitimate Expectations Arising out of Contractual Basis

An investor's legitimate expectations can arise out of a contract concluded with the state. Contracts are widely recognized as pillars of "legal stability and predictability" and thus present a good basis for legitimate expectations.[247] Nevertheless a pure breach of contractual obligations does not in itself amount to an automatic frustration of legitimate expectations. An additional factor is needed to amount to a breach of treaty obligations. As some author see it the additional factor would be "'a breach involving a sovereign power' (*pussiance publique*), or 'outright and unjustified repudiation of the transaction' or 'substantial breach' 'under certain limited circumstances. '"[248]

---

244 Potesta, Supra note 237, at 90.
245 *Id*, at 91.
246 The Oxford Handbook of International Investment Law, 496 (Peter Muchlinski, Federico Ortino & Christoph Schreuer eds., 2008)
247 Potesta, Supra note 237, at 101-2.
248 *Id.*, at 102.

b) Legitimate Expectations Arising out of Representations of State

A basis for legitimate expectations can be found in the promises and representations made by the state which the investor relied on, while making decisions regarding the investment.[249] However not all promises and representations give rise to legitimate expectations. Legitimate expectations in this case require a certain level of specificity. What is usually required is that the promise or representation is individualized and unambiguous. The promise must accordingly be addressed directly at the investor and not at the general public.[250]

c) Legitimate Expectations Arising out of State's Regulatory Framework

The investor can at times base its legitimate expectations on the state's regulatory and legislative framework at the time when it made its investment. The frustration of legitimate expectations can arise when the state changes its laws or the way they are applied. These changes need to bring economic loses to the investor. However, this approach is not commonly accepted in investment arbitration jurisprudence. The premise of such a wide interpretative approach lies in the dedication to stability envisaged by the treaty itself. Often the basis is found in the treaty language and when the Tribunals are willing to expand the interpretation of legitimate expectations. So, in which circumstances can legitimate expectations arise out of a requirement of the state not to change its laws? As some authors suggest a general reference to stability in the treaty language is insufficient to give rise to legitimate expectations. Only an explicit reference in the form of a "stability clause" should give rise to legitimate expectations. Furthermore, there can be no standardized "yardstick of good governance", rather the decision should be evaluated on a factual, case to case basis.[251] Some of the arbitral awards demonstrate how the standard should be evaluated. One Tribunal stated that legitimate expectations cannot exist where it is expected that the implementation, interpretation and application of the law has changed over time. Another Tribunal points to the

---

249 *Id.*, at 103.
250 *Id.*, at 105-6.
251 *Id.*, at 113.

"unreasonableness" of the changes in the law as something that might frustrate legitimate expectations.[252]

2. Legitimate Expectations under NAFTA

NAFTA article 1105 express connection to international law creates specific circumstances not found in other IIAs. Nevertheless, even despite the FTC's circumscribed seeing of the article, legitimate expectations have found their way into NAFTA investment arbitration jurisprudence. The case law demonstrates that legitimate expectations are observed as a part of the FET.

a) Thunderbird v. Mexico[253]

Thunderbird was the first case under NAFTA to fully investigate legitimate expectations, although *Metalclad v. Mexico* and other previous awards had previously touched upon the issue.[254]

Thunderbird is a game facilities operator. The company tried opening a business outpost in Mexico and received an opinion for operating such an establishment by the adequate state authority, confirming its legality.[255] However upon inspecting the establishment, Thunderbird was not allowed to continue its business. The authorities stated that the gaming machines were contrary to Mexico's gambling laws.[256] It was determined by the Mexican authorities and later confirmed by the Tribunal that Thunderbird did not truthfully disclose the functionality of the machines. They were characterized as "games of chance."[257] However Thunderbird claimed that its legitimate expectations were nevertheless frustrated.

---

252 *Id.*, at 117.
253 International Thunderbird Gaming Corp. v. Mexico, Award, (2007) available at: http://www.italaw.com/sites/default/files/case-documents/ita0431.pdf   (Visited last on Mar. 6, 2018) [herein after: *Thunderbird v. Mexico*].
254 Patrick Dumberry, THE PROTECTION OF INVESTORS' LEGITIMATE EXPECTATIONS AND THE FAIR AND EQUITABLE TREATMENT STANDARD UNDER NAFTA ARTICLE 1105, 31 (1) J. Int'l Arb. 47, 51 (2014).
255 *Thunderbird v. Mexico,* Supra note 253, § 55.
256 *Id,* §§ 73-4.
257 *Id,* §§ 151-53.

The Tribunal applied the following definition:

> "The concept of 'legitimate expectations' relates, within the context of the NAFTA framework, to a situation where a Contracting Party's conduct creates reasonable and justifiable expectations on the part of an investor (or investment) to act in reliance on said conduct, such that a failure by the NAFTA Party to honor those expectations could cause the investor (or investment) to suffer damages."[258]

The Tribunal held that the intentional failure to provide truthful information, on which the representation was based, cannot give rise to legitimate expectations. When the legality of the investment is doubtful there can be no legitimate expectations.[259]

b) Glamis Gold v. USA[260]

This NAFTA case was about a mining endeavor of a Canadian company, whose attempts at open pit mining were stopped by the state of California.[261]

The Tribunal considered legitimate expectations a constituent part of the FET standard. It set the legal standard for determining the threshold of legitimate expectations' violations:

> "Tribunal has explained in its discussion of the 1105 legal standard, a violation of Article 1105 based on the unsettling of reasonable, investment backed expectation requires, as a threshold circumstance, at least a quasi-contractual relationship between the State and the investor, whereby the State has purposely and specifically induced the investment."[262]

A strong message came out of this award as the Tribunal showed deference to the states right to regulate. Legitimate expectations for the Tribunal arise only when specific "quasi-contractual" representations are made to the investor. Even reasonable expectations made at the moment of

---

258 Id, § 147.
259 Dumberry, Supra note 254, at 51.
260 Glamis Gold, Ltd. v. USA, ICSID Award (2009) available at: http://www.italaw.com/sites/default/files/case-documents/ita0378.pdf (Visited last on Mar. 6, 2018) [herein after: *Glamis Gold v. USA*].
261 Dumberry, Supra note 254, at 54.
262 *Glamis Gold v. USA,* Supra note 260, § 766.

the investment should not be protected if there is no concrete representation.

c) Grand River v. USA[263]

In this case the Tribunal had to resolve an issue related to an economic burden imposed on foreign cigarette importers and distributors.[264]

The Tribunal addressed the issue of the relationship of external international law sources as a basis for the violation of a treaty standards. The interpretation set by FTC's Note was accordingly put into practice.[265] The Tribunal clearly rejected the importation of norms from other treaties in establishing standards for the violation of article 1105. It referred to the express linkage with international law and rejected the practice of "looking beyond". However, this rejection was aimed at establishing direct breaches of other international norms as direct violation of the investment treaty standards.[266] The Tribunal did not however dismiss the possibility to analyze the international sources of law as a matter of fact. Indeed, it entertained the possibility of other sources of law creating legitimate expectations but determined that, in the case itself, the legislation did not create legitimate expectations even if they had been pertinent to the case.[267]

d) Mobil v. Canada[268]

Mobil v. Canada was a case where the government of Canada implemented regulatory changes in relation to two companies in the business of off-

---

263 Grand River Enterprises Six Nations Ltd., et al. v. USA, ICSID Award (2011) available at: http://www.italaw.com/sites/default/files/case-documents/ita0384.pdf (Visited last on Mar. 6, 2018) [herein after: *Grand River v. USA*].
264 *Id*, §§ 18-19.
265 *Id*, § 176.
266 *Id*, § 219.
267 *Id*, §§ 141-142.
268 Mobil Investments Canada Inc. & Murphy Oil Corp. v. Canada, ICSID Decision on Liability and on Principles of Quantum, Case No. ARB(AF)/07/4 (2012) available at: http://www.italaw.com/sites/default/files/case-documents/italaw4399_0.pdf (Visited last on Mar. 6, 2018) [herein after: *Mobil v. Canada*].

shore oil drilling.[269] The measures required the companies to spend a certain percentage of their income on R&D, which they claimed violated their rights under the NAFTA Investment Chapter.[270]

In addressing the article 1105 issue, the Tribunal stated:

> "This applicable standard does not require a State to maintain a stable legal and business environment for investments, if this is intended to suggest that the rules governing an investment are not permitted to change, whether to a significant or modest extent. Article 1105 may protect an investor from changes that give rise to an unstable legal and business environment, but only if those changes may be characterized as arbitrary or grossly unfair or discriminatory."[271]

Likewise, the Tribunal created the standard which gave a "road map" for determining whether legitimate expectations were in fact frustrated. First of all, a clear representation needs to be made by the state to induce the investments. Second, the investor reasonably needs to rely on it. Third, the state must rescind on the representation.[272] The *Mobil* Tribunal thus took a very clear stance on how to approach regulatory changes in light of legitimate expectations.

3. Legitimate Expectations and Intellectual Property in Investment Arbitration

The relationship between legitimate expectations and the IPRs was up to very recently a matter of purely scholarly conjecture. However, cases started appearing that have addressed the issue.

a) Philip Morris v. Australia

The first case to establish a link between TRIPS, an international IP treaty, and an investment claim was the *Philip Morris v. Australia* case.

Australia enacted regulatory changes that require cigarettes to be sold in a particular type of packaging. This affected the way in which the trade-

---

269 *Id*, § 1.
270 *Id*, § 100.
271 *Id*, § 153.
272 *Id*, §152 (3).

mark of the cigarette brand could be displayed. The changes were implemented as a public health measure with a view of decreasing smoking.[273]

Philip Morris claimed that Australia had frustrated its legitimate expectations by failing to observe its international obligations from the TRIPS. It claimed that the measures unjustifiably encumbered its trademarks. Philip Morris claimed that it made the investment legitimately expecting Australia to comply with its international obligations.[274] However the Tribunal never got to addressing the legitimate expectations issue as the case was resolved by the Tribunal declining jurisdiction.[275]

Even though the investment claim did not succeed Australia still has to defend its legislation in an international forum. Currently there is an ongoing WTO case where the same plain packaging legislation was challenged under the TRIPS.[276] The outcomes remains to be seen.

b) Philip Morris v. Uruguay

So far, the only publicly available investment arbitration award that addressed the issue of legitimate expectations and IP laws is *Philip Morris v. Uruguay* case.

The factual background of the case is very similar to *Philip Morris v. Australia*. In 2005 Uruguay enacted regulatory changes affecting the tobacco industry.[277] The measures were envisaged as a public health measure to combat smoking.[278] Restrictions on advertising, mandatory health warnings, elevated taxation on tobacco products and banning smoking in public places were the steps the Uruguayan government undertook to fight smoking.[279] The claim put forward by Philip Morris was that Uruguay's measures affected their IPRs, which are under the Switzerland – Uruguay

---

273 *Philip Morris v. Australia,* Supra note 107, Australia's Response to Notice of Arbitration, §§ 20-23.
274 *Id,* §§ 6.5-6.8.
275 *Philip Morris v. Australia*, Supra note 107, Award, § 588.
276 The panel report is pending. *Australia — Certain Measures Concerning Trademarks, Geographical Indications and Other Plain Packaging Requirements Applicable to Tobacco Products and Packaging,* WT/DS467/20 (2013).
277 *Philip Morris v. Uruguay*, Supra note 107, Award, § 67.
278 *Id,* § 74-77.
279 *Id,* § 78.

BIT[280] protected as investments.[281] The measures in effect limited the way their registered trademarks are displayed.[282] Uruguay, as the respondent state, justified its measures on public policy grounds.[283]

The Tribunal agreed with Uruguay and recognized both the right of the state to regulate and the acceptable limits to regulation:

> "On this basis, changes to general legislation (at least in the absence of a stabilization clause) are not prevented by the fair and equitable treatment standard if they do not exceed the exercise of the host State's normal regulatory power in the pursuance of a public interest and do not modify the regulatory framework relied upon by the investor at the time of its investment "outside of the acceptable margin of change.""[284]

The Tribunal accepted the position that for legitimate expectations to arise a direct representation needs to be made by the state to the investor. Legislation directed at the general public cannot create legitimate expectations.[285] The Tribunal concluded that the manifest absence of a representation made by the state shows that there can be no legitimate expectations.[286] The Tribunal further recognized that the legislation which imposed the restrictions on Philip Morris' trademark rights were a legitimate policy measure. For these reasons the Tribunal dismissed the legitimate expectation claims of Philip Morris.[287]

The focus of the Tribunal was almost exclusively on the domestic legislation. The only time international treaties were mentioned in addressing this particular claim was as supporting proof for the justification of the measures undertaken by Uruguay.[288] Therefore international treaties were used merely for interpretative guidance. Even more importantly the treaties referred to, were not IP treaties.

---

280 The Agreement between the Swiss Confederation and the Oriental Republic of Uruguay on the Reciprocal Promotion and Protection of Investment, Oct. 7, 1988, 1976 U. N. T. S. 413.
281 *Philip Morris v. Uruguay*, Supra note 107, Award, § 9.
282 *Id*, § 11
283 *Id*, § 13.
284 *Id*, § 423.
285 *Id*, § 426
286 *Id,* § 429.
287 *Id*, § 432.
288 *Id,* § 423.

VI. Legitimate Expectations, Intellectual Property Rights and International Intellectual Property Law Framework – Eli Lilly and Beyond

A. Eli Lilly and Legitimate Expectations

So far there has been no other award in NAFTA jurisprudence that has address the relationship of international IP sources and legitimate expectations.[289] However from the analyzed case law some general principles can be extracted and applied to the circumstances of the *Eli Lilly* case, despite the case already being decided without fully addressing the issues related to legitimate expectations claims. There are several ways that Eli Lilly could have theoretically relied on the NAFTA IP Chapter as grounds for its legitimate expectations.

1. Customary International Law

Eli Lilly held that the "promise utility doctrine" is contrary to the generally accepted utility standard contained in the NAFTA IP Chapter. This argument can be used to determine violations of FET and legitimate expectations directly if it can be proved that the definition proposed has become part of contemporary customary international law or that it has become part of the customary international law standard for the protection of aliens. In these cases the Tribunal would be obliged to apply the law to the facts of the case. This standard was set by the *Mondev v. USA* Tribunal.[290] Even though Eli Lilly had tried to establish a uniformity of the utility standard[291], the fact that countries apply the standard differently[292] leads to the

---

289 The *Apotex* case which could have been the first one was decided on jurisdiction grounds. See, Apotex Holdings Inc. & Co. v. USA, ICSID Award, Case No. ARB(AF)/12/1, (2014) available at: http://www.italaw.com/sites/default/files/case-documents/italaw3324.pdf (Visited last on Mar. 6, 2018).

290 *Mondev v. USA,* Supra note 230.

291 Claimant's Post-hearing Brief, Supra note 112, §§ 136-37 & § 158.

292 Erstling, Samela & Woo, Supra note 191, at 12 (2012).

conclusion there is no standardized state practice or *opinio juris*.[293] Without the existence of the two fundamental requirements there can be no customary international law rule on patent utility which the Tribunal would be obliged to apply. Consequently, there could have been no basis for the establishment and violation of legitimate expectations in customary international law as well for Eli Lilly in the case.

2. Representations of State

As in the *Waste Management, Glamis Gold, Thunderbird and Mobil* the Tribunals have consistently held that for legitimate expectations to arise there needs to be a representation or conduct by the state, possibly in "quasi-contractual" form, on which the investor relied on to make its investment.

a) Patents as Representations of State

Patents confer particular rights to its right holder, which are guaranteed by the state.[294] Therefore a patent can be viewed as a representation made by the state.[295] Therefore only what is contained in the representation can create the basis for legitimate expectations.[296] The text of a granted Canadian patent states the following: "The present patent right grants its owner and to the legal representatives of its owner, for a term which expires twenty years from the filing date of the application in Canada, the exclusive right, privilege and liberty of making, constructing and using the invention and selling it to others to be used, subject to adjudication before any competent court of jurisdiction."[297]

---

293 State practice and *Opinio Juris* (The belief that states are legally obliged to follow the rule) are needed to establish rules of customary international law. See, Miles, Supra note 48, at 225.
294 Canadian Patent Act, Supra note 165, § 27 & § 2.1.
295 Eli Lilly has proposed this argument. See, Claimant's Reply, Supra note 124, § 360.
296 See *Mobil v. Canada*, Supra note 268,§ 152(3).
297 The text can be found on every front page of an issued hard copy of a Canadian patent. For example see, http://2innovative.net/wp-content/uploads/2015/05/Canadian_patent.jpg (Visited last on Mar. 6, 2018).

Very clearly the patent, as a representation of the state guarantees, offers no stability in relation to possible changes in the applicable law. The patent does not create any kind of link to international treaty standards. Even if the NAFTA is observed in isolation the patent gives no guarantee to the patent holder that the conduct of the state will be in line the NAFTA. Quite the contrary, it clearly points to the jurisdiction of Canadian law and courts. Even if the Tribunal acknowledges that a patent is a "quasi-contractual" document there should be a causal link between the "quasi-contract" and the requirement to keep a stable legislative framework or for the state to strictly adhere to its international obligations. A Canadian patent offers no such thing. The patent does not provide obligations for the state to implement a particular interpretation of the utility requirement. Therefore, the patent as such provides no grounds for legitimate expectations in relation to Canada's international obligations. In fact, the only thing that Eli Lilly could have legitimately expected is to use the inventions in a way prescribed by the text of the patent. Anything else would amount to an *ultra vires* act of interpretation.

b) Patentability Requirement Standards as Representations

Eli Lilly proposed the argument that the patentability standards are representations made by the state. "Unlike a law of general applicability, Canada's patentability standards, including its utility requirement, were technical regulations aimed, and relied upon, by a discrete and identifiable group."[298] This argument is far-fetched from the beginning. The practice of the NAFTA Tribunals requires that the representation is individualized.[299] Even though the patentability standards are relied on by a small number of persons they are still a part of the legislation aimed at the general public. Furthermore, the patentability standards do not point to any sources of international law and therefore cannot be used to establish international IP standards as grounds for legitimate expectations.

---

298 Claimant's Memorial, Supra note 126, § 284.
299 *Glamis Gold v. USA,* Supra note 260, § 766 & See *Mobil v. Canada,* Supra note 268, § 152(3).

3. Direct Application of International Intellectual Property Norms

The possibility of directly applying international IP norms is not allowed under the NAFTA jurisprudence. As set out by the FTC's Note and later confirmed by the *Grand River* Tribunal the breach of an external treaty, in this case the NAFTA IP Chapter, even though contained in the same wider agreement cannot automatically be a breach of the FET standard. Consequently, legitimate expectations cannot be established in such a way. The fact that there is no language in article 1105 that points to any kind of link with NAFTA IP Chapter, supports this reasoning.

Through the three situations mentioned it is clear that there can be no direct application of the NAFTA IP Chapter. There is no representation by the state that would let Eli Lilly rely on the NAFTA IP Chapter. Neither is the same Chapter and its standards part of customary international law. Nevertheless, the role of the NAFTA IP Chapter should not be entirely excluded.

The NAFTA IP Chapter can be used for interpretative guidance, with a prudently limited application scope. Such limitations could be inferred from the *S.D. Myers v. Canada* case where the Tribunal held that the breaches of article 1105 should be treated as a matter of international law but that the Tribunal should also show deference to domestic law and the state's right to regulate.[300]

4. "Arbitrary", "Grossly Unfair", "Unjust" or "Idiosyncratic" Changes in Law

In *Waste Management* and *Mobil* the Tribunals referred to the severity of change in the law that could frustrate legitimate expectations of the investor.[301] The change needed to justify the legitimate expectations claim needs to be "arbitrary", "grossly unfair", "unjust" or "idiosyncratic". However, the Tribunals have not offered a concrete definition of those terms. This is understandable as the standards set out by each of Tribunals were applied to the facts of the respective cases. Moreover, in the *Grand*

---

300 *S.D. Myers v. Canada*, Supra note 222, § 262.
301 *Waste Management v. Mexico*, Supra note 233, § 98. Likewise the Tribunal in *Mobile v. Canada* uses the term "grossly unfair". See, *Mobile v. Canada*, Supra note 268, § 153.

River case the Tribunal, even though rejecting the direct application of external treaties, went on to analyze them as possible grounds for legitimate expectations. It concluded that they do not form part of legitimate expectations.[302] This approach then leaves some room for the following possibility – the use of the NAFTA IP Chapter as a benchmark for determining "arbitrary", "grossly unfair", "unjust" or "idiosyncratic" changes in the law. The proposed analysis would function in the following way: The Tribunal needs a reference point to determine the "acceptable margin of change."[303] This reference point can be the NAFTA IP Chapter. The Tribunal should nevertheless limit its analysis exclusively to the text of the NAFTA IP Chapter. A Tribunal could therefore find a factor in determining the breach of article 1105 if the damage suffered by the investor resulted from a complete exclusion of the utility standard in national law or if the meaning of the utility requirement given in domestic law is blatantly contradictory or utterly irrational to the ordinary meaning of the word 'utility'. Any argument that provides a minimum of legal sense and rationality, which justifies the currently applicable law on the utility requirement, should be interpreted in favor of the respondent, keeping in mind the state's right to regulate. This can only be negated if the appropriate bodies, as set out in the NAFTA Institutional Arrangements and Dispute Settlement Procedures Chapter, would create a binding interpretation of the NAFTA IP Chapter, to which the domestic law is contrary. No such interpretation exists, and the benefit of the doubt should be given, for the previous reasons provided,[304] to the respondent state of Canada. Applying this formula, the Tribunal would have to conclude that the utility requirement, seen through the promise utility doctrine, does not create grounds for legitimate expectations based on (in)consistency with the NAFTA IP Chapter.

---

302 *Grand River v. USA*, Supra note 263, § 141.

303 Eli Lilly claims that the changes in Canadian patent law were outside of the "acceptable margin of change." See, Claimant's Memorial, Supra note 126, § 279.

304 See Chapter III for Canada's argumentation on the legitimacy and compliance of the utility requirement to international IP sources.

B. *Eli Lilly outside of NAFTA – International Investment Agreements and TRIPS as a Source of Legitimate Expectations*

Outside of the specific context of NAFTA there is a sea of different IIAs that protect IPRs as investments. Investors have the power to start investment arbitration proceedings and challenge their revoked patents, much like Eli Lilly has done. The TRIPS being the world's most important international IP treaty offers itself as a possible source of legitimate expectations. The relevance of the TRIPS for investors is not small as the share of assets in multinational companies consisting of intangible assets is on the rise.[305] However its role should, much like the role of the NAFTA IP Chapter in *Eli Lilly*, be limited.

The way an international treaty can be brought into investment arbitration is through one of the standards of protection provided in an IIA. Creating a link just by referencing the treaty to general rules of international law would not suffice.[306] Secondly a direct reference to an international IP treaty like the TRIPS in an IIA is problematic as well. Not only does article 23 of the DSU[307] confer the sole jurisdiction of WTO law to the WTO dispute settlement mechanism but the capability of the arbitrators to address a legal issue stemming from another body of law is also unsettling.[308] Albeit this approach is with all of the hurdles conceivable,[309] it is undesirable as it might lead to a paradoxical application of the law.[310]

However, there is little to prevent arbitration Tribunals looking at the TRIPS, even in instances where there is no express link between the ap-

---

305   The Oxford Handbook of International Investment Law, Supra note 246, at 380.

306   Henning Grosse Ruse-Khan, LITIGATING INTELLECTUAL PROPERTY RIGHTS IN INVESTOR-STATE ARBITRATION: FROM PLAIN PACKAGING TO PATENT REVOCATION, (Uni. Of Cambridge Faculty of Law Legal Studies Research Paper Ser., Paper No. 52/2014, 2014), 1, 22 http://papers.ssrn.com/sol3/papers.cfm?abstract_id=2463711 (Visited last on Mar. 6, 2018).

307   See DSU, Supra note 62, art. 23.

308   Bryan Mercurio, SAFEGUARDING PUBLIC WELFARE?—INTELLECTUAL PROPERTY RIGHTS, HEALTH AND THE EVOLUTION OF TREATY DRAFTING IN INTERNATIONAL INVESTMENT AGREEMENTS, 6 J. Int'l Econ. L., 252, 261 (2015).

309   Fola Adeleke, INVESTOR – STATE ARBITRATION AND THE PUBLIC INTEREST THEORY, Online Proceedings, Working Paper No. 2014/12, Soc. Int'l Econ. L., 1, 39-40 available at: http://www.ssrn.com/link/SIEL-2014-BernConference.html (Visited last on Mar. 6, 2018).

310   An investment Tribunal could determine a violation of a IIA treaty standard even if WTO would proclaim the measure legal.

propriate IIA and the TRIPS. The application of the TRIPS would therefore depend on the qualification of the FET clause. A narrow definition and a link to customary international law would thus render the TRIPS out of the scope of the clause.[311] In a case where the FET clause is broadly worded there might be some room for the TRIPS to play a role. It seems that there would be no objection for an investment Tribunal to consider the TRIPS as a rule of applicable law.[312] A limited jurisdiction does not mean a limited scope of applicable law.[313] Accordingly one way that an investor could use the TRIPS as a basis for legitimate expectations is if the host state has provided for a direct application of the treaty in its domestic legal system.[314] This can be done through legislation or through representations given to the investor. The other way TRIPS can be used in FET and legitimate expectation claims is if the Tribunal uses the TRIPS directly for the interpretation of the facts of the case or as an interpretative guidance for certain provisions of the IIA. This approach is based on the VCLT 31(3) (c) by using TRIPS as "relevant context" for the interpretation of IIA clauses.[315] However article 31(3)(c) VCLT prevents direct application of other international treaty norms to the facts of the case.[316] Since the only proper interpretation of WTO law rests in the hands of the dispute settlement mechanism the maneuver space is very small. So, what could the Tribunals do when looking at the TRIPS? When determining violations of legitimate expectations according to TRIPS they can see whether the measure is in compliance with TRIPS by checking the decisions of the WTO panels. If the panel has ruled that the particular measure had violated the TRIPS, and in a case where the Tribunal is persuaded or obliged to use the TRIPS, the Tribunal may determine there has been a breach of legitimate expectations. However, until there is uncertainty whether the measure is

---

311 Vanhonnaeker, Supra note 204, at 110-12.
312 An approach not applicable under NAFTA investment Tribunals. See, Simon Klopschinski, THE WTOs DSU ARTICLE 23 AS GUIDING PRINCIPLE FOR THE SYSTEMIC INTERPRETATION OF INTERNATIONAL INVESTMENT AGREEMENTS IN THE LIGHT OF TRIPs, J. Int'l Econ. L., 211, 222 (2016).
313 *Fragmentation of International Law: Difficulties Arising from the Diversification and Expansion of International Law*, Report by the Study Group of the International Law Commission, § 45 (2006) available at: http://legal.un.org/ilc/documentation/english/a_cn4_l682.pdf (Visited last on Mar. 6, 2018).
314 Klopschinski, Supra note 312, at 234.
315 *Id*, at 236.
316 Adeleke, Supra note 309, at 26.

contrary to the TRIPS, the Tribunal should give the benefit of the doubt to the respondent state and show deference to domestic law. This approach is more acceptable as not only does it allows clarity of the law stemming from the appropriate body, but that it reinvigorates and reinforces the legitimacy of the TRIPS. However even this approach should be carefully considered. Besides the situation mentioned earlier, where the state expressly creates a link to an international source of IP law, the states by not mentioning the TRIPS in IIAs have never actually agreed for it to be a part of that particular IIA. This approach would essentially impose on the states obligations to which it never adhered to in the first place.[317]

---

317 Vadi, Supra note 46, at 174.

VII. Is Conformity with International Intellectual Property Norms Enough?

This thesis has tried to demonstrate that the investment Tribunals should approach the interpretation and application of international IP sources carefully and in limited manner. The thesis has also recognized that conformity with the same international sources of law constitutes just one factor in determining the issues pertaining to legitimate expectations. So, the question remains whether showing a measure is not inconsistent with the international IP law treaty is enough to sway the Tribunal to dismiss it as grounds for legitimate expectations or should other factors be included? As proposed by some authors, IPRs should be perceived not purely from an investment law standpoint but they must be read "in conformity with constitutional rights, HRL and other principles of justice."[318] IPRs have been recognized as policy tools in international treaties in their own right.[319] The TRIPS expressly states in article 8: "Members may, in formulating or amending their laws and regulations, adopt measures necessary to protect public health and nutrition, and to promote the public interest in sectors of vital importance to their socio-economic and technological development, provided that such measures are consistent with the provisions of this Agreement."[320] This notion should be taken into account by the arbitrators. However, it seems that some justification is indeed warranted. Theoretically, even if a state complies with its international IP law obligations it might nevertheless be found in violation of the standards of protection found in an IIA.[321] Therefore justifying the measure on some other

---

318 Ernst-Ulrich Petersmann, THE JUDICIAL TASK OF ADMINISTERING JUSTICE IN TRADE AND INVESTMENT LAW AND ADJUDICATION, 4 (1) J. Int'l Dis. Sett., 5, 8 (2013).
319 Okediji, Supra note 5, at 1133.
320 TRIPS, Supra note 20, art. 8.
321 Ho, Supra note 196, at 222.

grounds is sometimes necessary.[322] Both in the *Eli Lilly v. Canada*[323] and the *Philip Morris v. Uruguay*[324] the changes in IP law were defended on public policy justifications. The Tribunal in the *Phillip Morris v. Uruguay* case has very much taken those goals into account.[325] As in any legal dispute the amounting of evidence coupled with prudent argumentation that serves the purposes of the disputing party is crucial. This is particularly important as the broad wording of IIA provisions leaves considerable room for the investment Tribunals to rule both ways.[326] Therefore any changes in IP law would have considerably stronger chances if they have a rational policy argument behind them.

---

322 Susan L. Karamanian, BALANCING INVESTOR PROTECTIONS, THE ENVIRONMENT AND HUMAN RIGHTS: THE PLACE OF HUMAN RIGHTS IN INVESTOR-STATE ARBITRATION, 17 Lewis & Clark L. Rev., 423, 432 (2013).
323 Canada justifies the patent utility requirement on the basis of innovation policy. See, Respondent's Rejoinder Memorial, Supra note 137, § 237.
324 *Philip Morris v. Uruguay*, Award, Supra note 107, §§ 74-77.
325 *Philip Morris v. Uruguay*, Award, Supra note 107, § 432.
326 Carloline Henckles, PROTECTING REGULATORY AUTONOMY THROUGH GREATER PRECISION IN INVESTMENT TREATIES: THE TPP, CETA AND TTIP, 19 J. Int't Econ. L., 27, 38 (2016).

VIII. Conclusions

This thesis tried to show that international IP treaties can be used as a basis for legitimate expectations but in a fairly limited manner. Not only is the establishment of the link between an IIA and an international IP treaty beset with problems but this link itself is in many ways undesirable. The thesis likewise endeavored to show that conferring power to investment Tribunals to rule on treaties and bodies of law which they might not be acquainted with can produce undesirable results. However, the role of international IP treaties should not be totally excluded in investment arbitration. Their application and definite interpretation should be encouraged in the proper fora. Therefore, when the investment Tribunals apply IP treaties as the "applicable law" they would not need to interpret the law themselves. By encouraging state to state dispute resolution through the appropriate mechanisms and adjudicatory bodies and by adopting the ensuing legal interpretations several things would be resolved. First of all, the international IP treaties and their interpretation will remain rightly in the domain of public international law and the states which they primarily address. This would ensure that the policy objectives of IP law are still respected. Moreover, by encouraging interpretation at the appropriate level the investment Tribunals will be able to get a "final product" in the form of a definite interpretation. Finally, by defining and respecting the limits of international IP law and international investment law, the legitimacy of both systems of law would be ensured.

List of Works Cited

Articles:

Adeleke, Fola, Investor–State Arbitration and the Public Interest Theory, Online Proceedings, Working Paper No. 2014/12, Soc. Int'l Econ. L., 1, (2014)

Bacalski, Juan, Mexico's Pharmaceutical Patent Dilemma and the Lessons of India, 23 Ariz. J. Int'l & Comp. L., 717, (2006)

Baker, Brook K. Et al, Corporate Power Unbound: Investor-State Arbitration of IP Monopolies on Medicines – Eli Lilly v. Canada and the Trans-Pacific Partnership Agreement, (Northeastern Pub. Law and Legal Theory Faculty Research Paper Ser., Paper No. 242, 2015) 1,

Bernasconi-Osterwalder, Nathalie, State-State Dispute Settlement in Investment Treaties, (IISD Best Practice Ser. 2014), 1,

Bijlmakers, Stephanie, Effects of Foreign Direct Investment Arbitration on a State's Regulatory Autonomy Involving the Public Interest, 23 Am. Rev. Int'l Arb. 245, (2012)

Billingsley, James, Eli Lilly and Company v. The Government of Canada and the Perils of Investor-State Arbitration, 20 Appeal 27 (2015)

Dreyfuss, Rochelle et al, From Incentive to Commodity to Asset: How International Law is Reconceptualizing Intellectual Property, 36 Mich. J. Int'l L. 557, (2014-2015)

Dumberry, Patrick, The Protection of Investors' Legitimate Expectations and the Fair And Equitable Treatment Standard under NAFTA article 1105, 31(1) J. Int'l Arb. 47, (2014)

Erstling, Jay, et al, Usefulness Varies by Country: The Utility Requirement of Patent Law in the United States, Europe and Canada, Faculty Scholarship Paper 3(1) Cybaris, 1, (2012)

Falconi, Adam, CETA: An Opportunity to Fix Canada's Broken Pharmaceutical Patent Linkage System, 27 I.P.J., 325, (2015) 158

Griffiths, Johnathan, On the Back of a Cigarette Packet: Standardized Packaging Legislation and the Tobacco Industry's Fundamental Right to Intellectual Property, 4 I. P. Q. 243, (2015)

Grosse Ruse-Khan, Henning, Litigating Intellectual Property Rights in Investor-State Arbitration: From Plain Packaging to Patent Revocation, (Uni. Of Cambridge Faculty of Law Legal Studies Research Paper Ser., Paper No. 52/2014, 2014), 1

Grosse Ruse-Khan, Henning, et al, Patentability of Pharmaceutical Inventions under TRIPS, Domestic Court Practice as a Test for International Policy Space, (Max Planck Institute for Innovation and Competition Research Paper Ser., Paper No. 16-02, 2016) 1,

Henckles, Carloline, PROTECTING REGULATORY AUTONOMY THROUGH GREATER PRECISION IN INVESTMENT TREATIES: THE TPP, CETA AND TTIP, 19 J. Int't Econ. L., 27, (2016)

Hicks Laurinda L., et al, CONVERGENCE OF NATIONAL INTELLECTUAL PROPERTY NORMS IN INTERNATIONAL TRADING AGREEMENTS, 2 Am. U. J. Int'l L. & Pol'y, 769, (1997)

Ho, Cynthia M., SHOULD ALL DRUGS BE PATENTABLE?: A COMPARATIVE PERSPECTIVE, 17 Vand. J. Ent. & Tech. L. 295, 340 (2015).

Humm, Vanessa, AMERICAN TRADE NEWS HIGHLIGHTS FOR SUMMER 2013, THE RISE OF THE INVESTOR – STATE SUIT AND THE CALL FOR REFORM, 5 Law & Bus. Rev. Am. 425, (2013)

Jaime, Margie-Lys, RELYING UPON PARTIES' INTERPRETATION IN TREATY-BASED INVESTOR-STATE DISPUTE SETTLMENT: FILLING THE GAPS IN INTERNATIONAL INVESTMENT AGREEMENTS, 46 Geo. J. Int'l L. 261, (2014-2015)

Kalicki, Jean, et al, FAIR, EQUITABLE AND AMBIGUOUS: WHAT IS THE FAIR AND EQUITABLE TREATMENT IN INTERNATIONAL INVESTMENT LAW?, 22(1) ICSID Rev. Foreign Invs't L. J., 24, (2007)

Karamanian, Susan L., *Balancing Investor Protections, the Environment and Human Rights: The Place of Human Rights in Investor-State Arbitration*, 17 Lewis & Clark L. Rev., 423, 432 (2013)

Klopschinski, Simon, THE WTOs DSU ARTICLE 23 AS GUIDING PRINCIPLE FOR THE SYSTEMIC INTERPRETATION OF INTERNATIONAL INVESTMENT AGREEMENTS IN THE LIGHT OF TRIPs, J. Int'l Econ. L., 211, (2016)

Liddell, Kathleen, et al, FAIR AND EQUITABLE TREATMENT AND JUDICIAL PATENT DECISIONS, 19 J. Int'l Econ. L., 145, (2016)

Mercurio, Bryan, AWAKENING THE SLEEPING GIANT: INTELLECTUAL PROPERTY RIGHTS IN INTERNATIONAL INVESTMENT AGREEMENTS, 15(3) J. Int't Econ. L., 871 (2012)

Mercurio, Bryan, *Safeguarding Public Welfare?*—INTELLECTUAL PROPERTY RIGHTS, HEALTH AND THE EVOLUTION OF TREATY DRAFTING IN INTERNATIONAL INVESTMENT AGREEMENTS, 6 J. Int'l Econ. L., 252, (2015)

Petersmann, Ernst-Ulrich, THE JUDICIAL TASK OF ADMINISTERING JUSTICE IN TRADE AND INVESTMENT LAW AND ADJUDICATION, 4(1) J. Int'l Dis. Sett., 5, (2013)

Potesta, Michele, LEGITIMATE EXPECTATIONS IN INVESTMENT TREATY LAW: UNDERSTANDING THE ROOTS AND THE LIMITS OF A CONTROVERSIAL CONCEPT, 28(1) ICSID - For. Inv. L.J., 88, (2013)

Okediji, Ruth L., IS INTELLECTUAL PROPERTY "INVESTMENT"? ELI LILLY V. CANADA AND THE INTERNATIONAL INTELLECTUAL PROPERTY SYSTEM, 35 U. Pa. J. Int'l L. 1211, 1219 (2013-2014)

Schreuer, Christoph, et al, AT WHAT TIME MUST LEGITIMATE EXPECTATIONS EXIST? in A Liber Amicorum: Thomas Wälde - Law Beyond Conventional Thought, 265, (Jacques Werner & Arif Hyder Ali 1st ed. 2009)

Siebrasse, Norman, HGS V. LILLY: HOW SOON IS TOO SOON TO PATENT?, 24 I. P. J., 41, (2011).

Snodgrass, Elizabeth, PROTECTING INVESTOR'S LEGITIMATE EXPECTATIONS: RECOGNIZ-ING AND DELIMITING THE GENERAL PRINCIPLE, 21(1) ICSID - For. Inv. L.J., 1, (2006)

Stone, Jacob, ARBITRAIRNESS, THE FAIR AND EQUITABLE TREATMENT STANDARD, AND THE INTERNATIONAL LAW OF INVESTMENT, 25(1) L.J.I.L., 77, (2012)

Taubman, Anthony, AUSTRALIA'S INTERESTS UNDER TRIPS DISPUTE SETTLEMENT: TRADE NEGOTIATIONS BY OTHER MEANS, MULTILATERAL DEFENSE OF DOMESTIC POLICY CHOICE, OR SAFEGUARDING MARKET ACCESS?, 9 Melb. J. Int'l L., 217, (2008)

Vadi, Valentina, TOWARDS A NEW DIALECTICS: PHARMACEUTICAL PATENTS, PUBLIC HEALTH AND FOREIGN DIRECT INVESTMENT, 5(1) NYU J. Intell. Prop. & Ent. L., 113, (2015)

Vadi, Valentina Sara, THROUGH THE LOOKING-GLASS: INTERNATIONAL INVESTMENT LAW THROUGH THE LENS OF PROPERTY THEORY, 8 Manchester J. Int'l Econ. L., 22, (2011)

Voon, Tania, et al, INTELLECTUAL PROPERTY RIGHTS IN INTERNATIONAL INVESTMENT AGREEMENTS: STRIVING FOR COHERENCE IN NATIONAL AND INTERNATIONAL LAW, (Melbourne Legal Studies Research Paper, Paper No. 675, 2013)

Cases:

Apotex Holdings Inc. & Co. v. USA, ICSID Award, Case No. ARB(AF)/12/1, (2014)

Apotex Inc. v. Wellcome Foundation Ltd., [2002] 4 SCR 153, 2002 SCC 77 (Can.)

Australia — Certain Measures Concerning Trademarks, Geographical Indications and Other Plain Packaging Requirements Applicable to Tobacco Products and Packaging, WT/DS467/20 (2013)

Eli Lilly & Co. v. Canada, ICSID, Case No. UNCT/14/2 (2012)

Eli Lilly & Co. v. Novopharm Ltd., [2011] FC 1288 (Can.)

Eli Lilly & Co. v. Teva Canada Ltd., [2011] FCA 220 (Can.)

Glamis Gold Ltd. v. USA, ICSID Award (2009)

Grand River Enterprises Six Nations Ltd., et al. v. USA, ICSID Award (2011)

International Thunderbird Gaming Corp. v. Mexico, Award (2007)

Metalclad Corp. v. Mexico Award, ICSID Case No. ARB(AF)/97/1 (2001)

Mobil Investments Canada Inc. & Murphy Oil Corp. v. Canada, ICSID Decision on Liability and on Principles of Quantum, Case No. ARB(AF)/07/4 (2012)

Mondev I'ntl Ltd. v. USA, ICSID (Additional Facility) Award, Case No. ARB(AF)/99/2 (2002)

Panel Report, Canada – Term of Patent Protection, WT/DS170/AB/R (2000)

Panel Report, United States-Section 110(5) of the U.S. Copyright Act, WT/DS160/R (2000)

Philip Morris Asia Ltd. v. Australia, PCA Case No. 2012-12 107 (2011)

Philip Morris Brands Sàrl et al. v. Uruguay, ICSID Case No. ARB/10/7 (2009)

Pope & Talbot Inc. v. Canada, Award on the Merits of Phase II (2001)

S.D. Myers Inc. v. Canada Partial Award (2004)

Waste Management Inc. v. Mexico, ICSID (Additional Facility) Award, Case No. ARB(AF)/00/3 (2004)

Legislative Materials:

1994: General Agreement on Tariffs and Trade 1994, Apr. 15, 1994, Marrakesh Agreement Establishing the World Trade Organization, Annex 1A, THE LEGAL TEXTS: THE RESULTS OF THE URUGUAY ROUND OF MULTILATERAL TRADE NEGOTIATIONS 17 (1999), 1867 U.N.T.S. 187

2012 U.S. Model Bilateral Investment Treaty, Treaty Between The Government of the United States of America and the Government Of [Country] Concerning The Encouragement and Reciprocal Protection of Investment (2012)

Agreement on Trade-Related Aspects of Intellectual Property Rights, Apr. 15, 1994, Marrakesh Agreement Establishing the World Trade Organization, Annex 1C, THE LEGAL TEXTS: THE RESULTS OF THE URUGUAY ROUND OF MULTILATERAL TRADE NEGOTIATIONS 320 (1999), 1869 U.N.T.S. 299, 33 I.L.M. 1197

Agreement between the Swiss Confederation and the Oriental Republic of Uruguay on the Reciprocal Promotion and Protection of Investment, Oct. 7, 1988, 1976 U. N. T. S. 413

Berne Convention for the Protection of Literary and Artistic Works, Sep. 9, 1886, 331 U.N.T.S. 217

Constitution Act, 1867, § 91(22), 30 & 31 Vict. Ch. 3 (U. K.), *as reprinted in* R.S.C., No. 5 (Appendix 1985)

Convention on the Recognition and Enforcement of Foreign Arbitral Awards, Jun 10, 1958, 330 U.N.T.S.

Copyright Act of 1976, 17 U.S.C. (2012)

General Agreement on Trade in Services, Apr. 15, 1994, Marrakesh Agreement Establishing the World Trade Organization, Annex 1B, THE LEGAL TEXTS: THE RESULTS OF THE URUGUAY ROUND OF MULTILATERAL TRADE NEGOTIATIONS 284 (1999), 1869 U.N.T.S. 183

German Model Treaty-2008, Treaty between the Federal Republic of Germany and ... concerning the Encouragement and Reciprocal Protection of Investments (2008)

International Centre for Settlement of Investment Disputes (ICSID), Rules of Procedure for the Institution of Conciliation and Arbitration Proceedings, Mar. 18, 1965, ICSID/15/Rev. 1 (2003)

North American Free Trade Agreement, U.S.-Can.-Mex., Dec. 17, 1992, 32 I.L.M. 289 (1993)

Notes of Interpretation of Certain Chapter Eleven Provisions (Free Trade Commission, July 31, 2001)

OECD, The Multilateral Agreement on Investment Draft Consolidated Text, DAFFE/ MAI(98)7/REV1 (1998)

Paris Convention for the Protection of Industrial Property, Mar. 20, 1883, 21 U.S.T. 1583, 828 U.N.T.S. 305

Patent Act, § 2, R.S.C., c. P-4 (Can.)

Patents (Amendment) Act, § 3(d), No. 15 of 2005, India Code (2005)

Treaty between the Federal Republic of Germany and Pakistan for the Promotion and Protection of Investment, Ger.-Pak., Nov. 25, 1959, 457 U.N.T.S. 24

UNCITRAL Arbitration Rules, Dec. 15, 1976, 15 I. L. M. 701 (1976)

Understanding on Rules and Procedures Governing the Settlement of Disputes, Marrakesh Agreement Establishing the World Trade Organization, Annex 2, THE LEGAL TEXTS: THE RESULTS OF THE URUGUAY ROUND OF MULTILATERAL TRADE NEGOTIATIONS 354 (1999), 1869 U.N.T.S. 401

Vienna Convention on the Law of Treaties, *opened for signature* May 23, 1969, 1155 U.N.T.S. 331

Books:

DOLZER, RUDOLF, ET AL, PRINCIPLES OF INTERNATIONAL INVESTMENT LAW, 1st ed. (2008)

DRAHOS, PETER, ET AL, INFORMATION FEUDALISM, WHO OWNS THE KNOWLEDGE ECONOMY, (2002)

GERVAIS, DANIEL, THE TRIPS AGREEMENT: DRAFTING HISTORY AND ANALYSIS, 3rd ed. (2008)

FOLSOM, RALPH. H., NAFTA, FREE TRADE AND FOREIGN INVESTMENT IN THE AMERICAS IN A NUTSHELL (2014)

FOLSOM, RALPH H., PRINCIPLES OF INTERNATIONAL TRADE LAW (2014)

HORNER, JESSI J., CANADIAN LAW AND THE CANADIAN LEGAL SYSTEM (2007)

JUDGE, ELIZABETH F., ET AL, INTELLECTUAL PROPERTY: THE LAW IN CANADA, (2011)

KRATZ, MARTIN P.J. Q.C., CANADA'S INTELLECTUAL PROPERTY LAW IN A NUTSHELL, 2nd ed., 202 (2010)

KLÄGER, RONALD, 'FAIR AND EQUITABLE TREATMENT' IN INTERNATIONAL INVESTMENT LAW (2011)

MILES, KATE, THE ORIGINS OF INTERNATIONAL INVESTMENT LAW, EMPIRE, ENVIRONMENT AND THE SAFEGUARDING OF CAPITAL (2013)

PASTOR, ROBERT A., THE NORTH AMERICAN IDEA, THE VISION OF A CONTINENTAL FUTURE (2011)

PERRY, STEPHEN J., ET AL, CANADIAN PATENT LAW, 2nd ed. (2014)

SCHILL, STEPHAN W., THE MULITILATERIZATION OF INTERNATIONAL INVESTMENT LAW (2009)

SOUTH CENTER, The TRIPs Agreement, A Guide for the South, The Uruguay Round Agreement on Trade-Related Intellectual Property Rights (2000)

The Oxford Handbook of International Investment Law, (Peter Muchlinski, Federico Ortino & Christoph Schreuer eds., 2008)

VAN DEN BOSSCHE, PETER, THE LAW AND POLICY OF THE WORLD TRADE ORGANIZATION, 2nd ed. (2010)

VANHONNAEKER, LUKAS, INTELLECTUAL PROPERTY RIGHTS AS FOREIGN DIRECT INVESTMENTS: FROM COLLISION TO COLLABORATION (2015)

Other:

Fair and Equitable Treatment, UNCTAD Series On Issues In International Investment Agreements II, (2012)

Fragmentation of International Law: Difficulties Arising from the Diversification and Expansion of International Law, Report by the Study Group of the International Law Commission, (2006)

The Role of International Investment Agreements in Attracting Foreign Direct Investment to Developing Countries, UNCTAD Series on International Investment Policies for Development, (2009)

Webistes:

Treaty Protection for Global Patents: A Response to a Growing Problem for Multinational Pharmaceutical Companies, Jones Day Publications (2012) available at: http://www.jonesday.com/treaty_protection/